A Tribute to
Woody Guthrie & Leadbelly

Teacher's Guide

by
Will Schmid

Credits

Photos:

Unit 2: Courtesy of the Library of Congress Folklife Division, California WPA collection.

Unit 3: Courtesy of the Library of Congress Photographic Archives, John and Alan Lomax collection.

Page design, typesetting, engraving and editing by Will Schmid in cooperation with MENC staff.

Copyright © 1991
Music Educators National Conference
1902 Association Drive, Reston, Virginia 22091
All rights reserved.
Printed in the United States of America
ISBN 0-940796-85-6

Table of Contents

Foreword

The most modern music often reveals deep roots in earlier traditions, and this set of teaching materials stresses long-term cultural continuities as well as artistic production. These materials focus on the creativity and power of preindustrial music and on its enduring influence on contemporary popular music. Traditional music is homemade by people whose styles and repertoires draw from their families and their communities. Both Woody Guthrie and Leadbelly—whose songs are featured here—were traditional musicians who had a strong influence on popular music.

I encourage you as an educator to take a do-it-yourself approach to these materials, so that, from this generation of students, the next Leadbellys and Woody Guthries can step forward. Among your students are members of future Sweet Honey in The Rock ensembles, future Bob Dylans, and future producers and documentarians of our continuing American creativity.

Use these materials to teach about the passion with which Woody and Leadbelly wrote. It is an infectious passion, full of love for the variety, the creativity, and the rights of humankind. Use the rich citations of their ideas in prose, poetry, and song to sow musical seeds on the fertile ground. You will motivate some students to dig deeply into the bibliographic and discographic materials in this set of lessons. As a teacher, you can encourage local libraries to acquire materials presently unavailable in your school or public collections. If your students find themselves in these books, recordings, and this video tape, you will have kindled fires that will burn long after our time.

My suggestions stem from certain unique experiences of my musical life. First I had the privilege of knowing and learning from Woody Guthrie in New York's Washington Square Park—it was Woody who inspired me to take up the mandolin. And second, I learned about our grass roots traditions from the John and Alan Lomax 78-rpm field recordings at the Library of Congress.

During my college years in the fifties, I was swept up into the folk-song movement. Leadbelly had already passed on, but his music was everywhere. Once out of school, I played bluegrass as a member of the Greenbriar Boys; we recorded and toured with Joan Baez. During the years that followed, I watched a teenager named Bob Dylan come into the New York folk scene, learn from Guthrie's recordings, and begin to emerge as an influential song writer and stylist himself.

As a young, nonacademic field-worker, I turned my sights from the urban revival to country tradition and recorded an Appalachian string band, which featured an old-timer who had recorded commercially in the twenties.[1] Accompanying him was a much younger, brilliant guitar player/singer who clearly deserved a broader audience. I edited my field tapes, wrote carefully researched notes, and persuaded Folkways Records, Inc. to issue the material.[2]

Having difficulty in finding an impresario for these musicians, I decided to manage them myself; and now, thirty years later, that brilliant Appalachian musician—Doc Watson—is known around the world. As I worked with Doc, Bill Monroe, the founder of bluegrass music, came to mind.[3] He was then struggling against the impact of Elvis and rock and roll. I moved to Nashville to manage both Doc Watson and Bill Monroe and introduced them to the urban college audiences already familiar with the Greenbriar Boys and Joan Baez.

Moving from recordings and management to festivals and administration, I did fieldwork and production for the Newport Folk Festival.

Later, it became possible to establish the Smithsonian Festival of American Folklife, an annual tribute to grass roots music and material culture now produced by the Smithsonian Institution's Office of Folklife Programs.[4]

The *A Vision Shared* album and video tape grew out of a conversation I had with Bob Dylan and out of his ensuing commitment to help the Smithsonian purchase the collection and the rights to Folkways Records and the Woody Guthrie archives. Dylan asked CBS to co-produce the recording with the Smithsonian and persuaded his colleagues to record Woody's and Leadbelly's songs, donating their royalties to the Smithsonian. The companion recording, *The Original Vision*, draws on the archives acquired by the Institution with the purchase of Folkways Records, Inc.[5]

In short, I write as a do-it-yourself musician with experience in the folk-song movement that stretches from the early fifties to the present. Based on this experience, I am confident that your students can find a variety of ways in which to begin their own exciting experience with traditional folk music. Invite them to seek out local musicians and to learn from them. Assist them in creating and improvising from their own experiences. Bring the rich and diverse repertoire of traditional music, both secular and sacred, into your classrooms—it is still alive in communities across our nation. The more background you can present to your students, the more energy you will generate in them. So use this material to "bring it all back home."

Ralph Rinzler
Assistant Secretary Emeritus
Smithsonian Institution

Notes

1. Re-released on *Anthology of American Folk Music* (Folkways 2951).

2. *Old Time Music at Clarence Ashley's— Volumes 1 and 2* (Smithsonian/Folkways SF40029, Folkways 2355, 2359). For another, more recent recording, listen to *The Watson Family* (Smithsonian /Folkways SF40012).

3. Listen, for example, to *The High Lonesome Sound, Bluegrass Instrumentals* (Decca; MCA MCAC-11OE).

4. If you cannot find some of the reference materials cited in this teacher's guide or in the student text, write to the Smithsonian/Folkways Archives, Smithsonian Institution, Washington, DC 20560 or to the American Folklife Center, Library of Congress, Washington, DC 20540.

5. The *A Vision Shared* video tape, cassettes, and compact discs and *The Original Vision* cassettes and compact discs are available from MENC Publication Sales, 1902 Association Drive, Reston, VA 22091.

How to Use This Book

The *Tribute to Woody Guthrie and Leadbelly Teacher's Guide* is a practical resource for how to use the *Student Text*, the *A Vision Shared* video tape and recording, and *The Original Vision* recording.

Who Is It For?

The Student Text and Teacher's Guide suggestions are intended for use with the following types of classes:

- **4th and 5th grade classes**—studying American music, culture and history; for use with elementary choruses (who sing harmony by ear); for use as source material for a homemade musical about Woody Guthrie or Leadbelly.

- **middle school general music**—will work well in units on folk and popular music, American music, guitar, Autoharp, listening, 6th grade world cultures, or multicultural education.

- **high school general music**—for courses in music appreciation (listening), guitar, folk and popular music, music in our lives, folk instrument labs, American history, or any form of multicultural education.

- **adult continuing education**—for experiences with guitar, American folk and popular music, folk instruments, Autoharp, American history or sociology

Teaching strategies suggested throughout this book should be adapted to the needs and interests of the students who use it.

What Does It Include?

The Teacher's Guide is laid out according to this format:

- **Page numbers** are given at the bottom of the Teacher's Guide pages as **TG-XX** to avoid possible confusion with the Student Text pages.

- **Student Text pages for Units 1-3** (with the exception of full-page photos) appear on left-facing pages. Notice that the original Student Text page number is given in the upper right-hand corner of the page. Student Text pages for Unit Four are not included in this book.

- **Teacher's Guides for each Student Text page** appear on the right-facing page opposite their appropriate Student Text page. Each Teacher's Guide page includes:
  - Objectives
  - Teaching strategies for:
    - Listening
    - Performing (singing and playing)
    - Describing (discussing, thinking)
    - Creating (composing, improvising)
  - Assessment
  - Resources for additional study:
    - Books
    - Recordings
    - Films and videos
- **Teacher's Guide for Student Text Songs** contains suggestions for:
  - Singing and playing the songs
  - Instrumental accompaniments
  - Strategies for each song in the Student Text. (The Woody Guthrie and Leadbelly songs appear only in the Student Text.)

- **Teacher's Guide Masters #1 - 15** may be duplicated in any form (including as a transparency) for use by your class. The Masters include:
  - Supplementary songs
  - Lyrics
  - Listening charts
  - Quizzes (with Keys for the teacher—just cut off the answers before duplicating)

How Should It Be Used?

Take a tip from Ralph Rinzler's Foreword and use the combined book, video, and audio resources to bring the music into the lives of your students in some of the following ways:

- **Use the *A Vision Shared* video tape to stimulate interest.** The new generation of singers and songwriters breathe fresh life into the great songs of Woody Guthrie and Leadbelly. You may wish to use the video in small doses rather than playing the whole thing all at once.

- **Sing, play and study the songs from the Student Text.** Put as much life into these songs as you can by—
  - playing solid rhythmic accompaniments (even some that sound like rock).
  - encouraging students to create their own versions (just like the performers on the video tape).
  - writing new verses or new songs
  - finding other songs on the same topics
  - discussing what the songs are about. Topics such as racism and the homeless are major topics for today.
  - comparing the versions on *The Original Vision* recording with those in the Student Text and the video tape.

- **Keep classes interesting by keeping students active.** Use the reading from the Student Text as a prelude to activities or projects. Give students a reading focus by asking them to look for specifics. The **Learning Objectives**, **Vocabulary**, and the **Unit Review** at the beginning and end of units may help.

- **Use these materials as a springboard to helping students make music their own.** Help them use music as a positive force in their lives—through creating, performing and listening.

- **Have students read the biographies in Unit Four—The New Generation.** Read these sections as you watch and listen to the *A Vision Shared* video tape or recording. Encourage them to dig further into the lives and music of these performers.

- **Let Woody Guthrie and Leadbelly stimulate a new age of social concern** —for the environment, for social and economic justice, for racial understanding and equality, and for a world that badly needs to learn to live in peace.

These coordinated learning materials present you and your students with the opportunity to have a great time while a lot of worthwhile learning takes place. The books, video tape and recordings can be the key that unlocks the door to the magical power of creative music making in the lives of your students. And finally, these materials should help you teach in a more vital way and come to a deeper understanding of American folk and popular music.

Will Schmid

Will Schmid

1.

African and European Roots of American Music

LEARNING OBJECTIVES

After reading UNIT ONE and doing the activities you will be able to:

• Describe how songs become folk songs through oral tradition and variation.

• List contributions to American music made by Africans and Europeans.

• Identify elements of African and European musical style in popular recordings.

• Describe how "chart hits" sometimes turn into folk music.

• Identify types of music created by African- and European-Americans over the last 200 years.

• Write your own parodies—new words to old tunes.

VOCABULARY

Autoharp	Hillbilly
Ballad	Jazz
Banjo	Lyrics
Blues	Oral tradition
Broadside	Parody
Call and response	Popular song
Country & western	Race records
Cover recording	Ragtime
Fiddle	Rhythm & blues
Folk song	Spiritual
Gospel	Syncopation
Guitar	Work song
Gutbucket	Variation
Harmony	Zither

In UNIT ONE you will learn how Africans and Europeans brought their music to America and how these root traditions combined and grew into many different musical styles. Long before African- and European-Americans learned to live together with any sense of equality, they were attracted by each other's music and to the music of other cultural groups. Who knows how large a contribution music has made in creating a world where people live in mutual respect?

People make new songs in a variety of ways—some write them down and some work orally (or aurally, by ear). Once created, songs take on a life of their own. Some change to suit the times or the singer, some stubbornly remain the same, and some simply disappear. In listening to the *A Vision Shared* recording or video tape, you will hear how popular singers have brought music born of an oral tradition into the modern world of recorded music. In this unit you will learn how these forces work and how songs have changed to reflect America's history.

> *I usually figure a song that I compose is like a child; mine to control only as long as it sticks around the house. When it goes out into the world, it grows and has a life of its own, or maybe dies . . . in the long run, it is those who listen to the song throughout the world who will decide which version will last, and which will be forgotten.*
>
> —Pete Seeger

LISTEN

Since Unit One tells the story of how European and African musical elements combined in a unique way to make the many American musical styles, you may wish to begin by finding out what your students already know about this subject. Here are some sample questions and strategies that will get the process started.

•Which musical instruments originally came from Africa and which came from Europe? [For examples, see the lists on TG-17 and TG-19.]

•Are the following American musical styles **more heavily influenced** by African (A) or European (E) music? Be sure to point out that each style is usually a mixture of influences.

PERFORM

jazz – A

country – E

rock – A

blues – A

spirituals – A for African-American spirituals; E for Sacred Harp spirituals

ballads – E

DESCRIBE

gospel – A for African-American gospel; E for white gospel

soul – A

bluegrass – E

•Can you tell if singers are African-American or European-American by the way they sing? [No] Is singing style a genetic trait? [No] Can members of one race or culture learn to sing in the style of another culture? [Yes]

CREATE

You may find that these questions will promote lively discussion. Challenge students to find examples of singers from one culture who sing in another style. [For example, Charley Pride (African American) sings in a convincing white country style; Phil Driscoll (European American) sings in a convincing black gospel style.

•Have students list style characteristics they would expect to hear on recordings of either **African-American** or **European-American** singers. [For examples, see the Style Chart on TG-56.]

RESOURCES

Books

The New Grove Dictionary of American Music. 4 vols. New York: Macmillan, 1986.

The New Grove Dictionary of Jazz. 2 vols. New York: Macmillan, 1988.

The New Grove Dictionary of Musical Instruments. 3 vols. New York: Macmillan, 1984.

Recordings

Anthology of American Folk Music. Folkways 2951-53. This important anthology, available from the Smithsonian, features landmark recordings by Blind Lemon Jefferson, the Carter Family, Maybelle Carter, and many others mentioned throughout this text.

Oral Tradition and Folk Music

Once music is created, it is usually shared with other people. In sharing a song or instrumental piece, the music often changes. Music changes more when it is not written down and is passed from person to person by word of mouth—a process called **oral tradition**. In this section you will see how oral tradition has affected American music and created a type of music called **folk music**.

When Words Change

Sometimes musical **lyrics** (words) change because they are misunderstood. Have you ever taken a phone message and written down a stranger's name with a highly original spelling? Perhaps you heard a rock song and thought the singer was singing one thing, only to find out later that it was something else. For example, there is the classic story of the person who thought "The Star Spangled Banner" began "José, can you see?"

Composers sometimes put new words to an old tune. The result is often called a **parody** or **take-off**. Think of the many songs you know that have several different sets of words. Here are a few examples to start your list:

"On Top of Old Smokey" → "On Top of Spaghetti"

"When Johnny Comes Marching Home" → "Ants Go Marching"

"Greensleeves" → "What Child Is This"

People make up new words to suit the needs of the moment, whether poking fun at a political candidate, writing a religious song, protesting an environmental problem, or just having a good time. When the printing press was invented around 1450, people started printing new words to songs called **broadsides** and selling them in the streets. Today, if you go to a meeting and receive a sheet with new words to an old song you are getting a modern-day broadside.

Ballads (story songs) came from Europe and exist in many different **variations** with different sets of verses. You know what happens when a rumor starts going around school—it often results in wild stories that have little to do with truth. The oral tradition works in this same way with ballad lyrics. In the process of making a ballad his or her own, a singer might personalize it by changing the location or the names of the main characters. Sometimes singers forget the original words and are forced to make up some new ones on the spot while they are singing. When this happens, they sometimes borrow words from other songs with a similar story line. Below are examples of similar lines that appear in various English ballads when someone is about to die.

> O mother, O mother, go dig my grave,
> Go dig it wide and deep;
>
> O father, O father go dig my grave,
> Go dig it deep and narrow;
>
> O mother, O mother, go make my bed,
> And fix it wide and smooth;
>
> Go dig my grave both wide and deep,
> A marble stone at my head and feet;

In the African-American tradition, words are often improvised as part of a **call and response** form where the leader makes up a line and the rest of the group answers with a repeated response. This form was used in both **work songs** and **spirituals**. A typical example comes from the song "Wade in the Water," which uses a common two-line rhyming structure.

> Look at those children dressed in white,
> Wade in the water,
> Must be the children of the Israelite.
> Wade in the water.
>
> Look at those children dressed in red,
> Wade in the water,
> Must be the children that Moses led.
> Wade in the water.

See examples of these two-line rhythming verses in Leadbelly's "Rock Island Line" (page 42). This same two-line structure carries over into the **blues**, but the first line is repeated to make an AAB rhyme scheme.

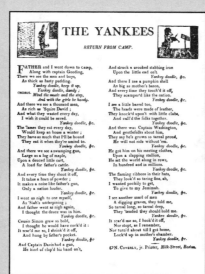

18th century Revolutionary War broadside

✔ Students will learn how **oral tradition** works in both the African- and European-American musical traditions.

LISTEN

The Oral/Aural Tradition Game

•Select 3 volunteer students to step out into the hall while the rest of the class listens carefully (without song sheets) to a version of the English ballad "The Golden Vanity" (Master #1, TG-50) sung by the teacher or a student.

•Select a student in the classroom to retell the ballad story from memory to one student who is brought in from the hall. Don't allow questions, and urge students to listen carefully.

•Repeat this process 2 more times as the hearer becomes storyteller to another student brought in from the hall.

PERFORM

•Sing (or listen to) the song again using copies of the music. Ask students to identify what elements changed in each retelling of the ballad story.

•Find out if students know any stories about misunderstood words that are a result of the oral/aural tradition.

New Words to an Old Tune

•Start by singing some versions of the most parodied American song of all time—"The Battle Hymn of the Republic." Before passing out the song sheets, hum through the tune, and then ask how many different sets of words students know to this song. When you have exhausted the versions the class knows, pass out copies of Master #2 (TG-51), and sing these versions.

DESCRIBE

•Ask students what other parodies they know. Sing several as time permits.

•Have students pick a melody that almost everyone knows; then have them make up their own set of words to it. Share the results with the class by singing (student solos or as a class) through all or some of the parodies.

European-American Ballad Characteristics

CREATE

•Explore the world of European-influenced ballads by looking for common characteristics such as **stock openings**, **stock lines** (See "dig my grave" examples), **repeated last lines** to involve audience, or **enculturation**—the story reinforces the values of society (Compare to the soaps or fairytales.).

African-American Two-Line Rhymes

•Sing and/or listen to some of the typical 2-line rhymes found in spirituals such as "Wade in the Water" and "It May Be the Last Time" (Master #4, TG-53).

•Have students make up rhyming lines using colors such as:
Look at those children dressed in _____, (Add 2nd line.)

RESOURCES

Books

Bronson, Bertrand. *The Singing Tradition of Child's Popular Ballads.* Princeton, NJ: Princeton University Press, 1976.

Lomax, Alan. *Folksongs of North America in the English Language.* New York: MacMillan, 1965.

Grissom, Mary Allen. *The Negro Sings a New Heaven.* New York: Dover Publications, 1969.

Recordings

Jean Redpath. Philo 2015 [Scottish ballad singer].

Joan Baez Ballad Book. 2 vols. Vanguard 73107, 73115.

Variants and Versions of Barbara Allen. Library of Congress AAFS L54.

Both Woody Guthrie and Leadbelly borrowed old tunes to make new songs. Both "Ramblin' 'Round" and "Roll On, Columbia" (page 47) are new words written to the tune of "Goodnight Irene" (page 36).

When Music Changes

A twenty-verse song can become rather boring if the melody is sung exactly the same each time. Good singers see to it that this does not happen by working subtle variations into the melody of some verses. You can make melody variations by changing the rhythm, changing some of the pitches in the melody, or by adding ornamentation. Listen to the different versions of "This Land Is Your Land" as good examples of melody variation and individual singing on the *A Vision Shared* video tape or recording.

Ballads sometimes retain the basic story but have many different melodies. Here are the beginnings of three different variations of the broadside ballad "Froggie Went A-Courtin'." Notice how different the melodies are:

Example 1

The frog went court - in' and he did ride, a - huh,

Example 2

Frog went a - court - in' and he did ride,

Example 3

The frog went court - in' and he did ride,

The African-American call and response form gives the song leader an opportunity to improvise new melodies. This adds variety to the music and gives energy to the group singing the response. You can hear this improvisation in worksongs, spirituals, gospel, blues, and jazz. Listen to Sweet Honey in The Rock sing Leadbelly's call and response song, "Gray Goose," on the *A Vision Shared* recording.

From Sheet Music to Folk Song

A **popular song** written by a composer usually becomes a piece of sheet music. If the song is sung by enough people, it becomes part of oral tradition and results in the kinds of variations you have just studied. When a song is part of oral tradition for a long enough period of time, people call it a **folk song**.

In 1838 the number-one popular song of the year was "Rosin the Beau." Below is the original sheet music cover and some of the parodies that followed during the 19th century.

OLD ROSIN THE BEAU

Favourite Comic Song

Dedicated with much respect

to the members of the

FALCON BARGE

by the Publisher.

Arranged by

J. C. BECKELL.

PHILADELPHIA.

Osbourn's Music Salon N.O. 112 St.

1838 – original words	I live for the good of my nation, And my sons are all growing low; But I hope that the next generation Will resemble old Rosin the Beau.
1840 – the first U.S. Presidential campaign where songs and slogans played a big part.	You can't make a song to Van Buren, Because his long name will not do; There's nothin' about him allurin', As there is about Tippecanoe!
1860 – a version that helped to elect Abraham Lincoln President.	Hurrah for the choice of the nation! Our chieftain so brave and so true; We'll go for the great Reformation— For Lincoln and Liberty too!
late 19th century – "Acres of Clams" – how a man moved west and settled in Puget Sound.	I've traveled all over this country, Prospecting and digging for gold. I've tunneled, hydraulicked and cradled, And, I have been frequently sold.

The process of turning popular sheet music into parodies continues into the 1990's as popular songs are reworked to become radio and television commercials. Find some examples.

LISTEN

✔ Students will discriminate differences in **melodic variations** when listening to contrasting recordings of the same song.

Melodic Variation

•Play several different recordings of the same song to show how each singer makes a song his or her own. Some good examples would be:

"Let It Be" —The Beatles or Aretha Franklin

"Bridge Over Troubled Water" —Simon & Garfunkel or Aretha Franklin

"Hard Rain's A-Gonna Fall" —Bob Dylan or Joan Baez

"All Along the Watchtower" —Bob Dylan or Jimi Hendrix

PERFORM

•Compare the Guthrie and Leadbelly melodies from the song sheets (pp. 31-47 in Student Text) and *The Original Vision* recording to the versions done by contemporary singers on *A Vision Shared.*

•Examine the art of melodic variation within a song. To provide variety, singers often vary the melody from verse to verse. A good example of this occurs in Little Richard's version of "Rock Island Line" on *A Vision Shared.* Point out that Woody Guthrie rarely sang the melody of his own songs the same way twice.

•Challenge students to take one of the songs from the Student Text and compose some melodic variations of their own.

DESCRIBE

✔ Students will be able to describe the process through which a **popular** song sometimes turns into a **folk** song.

Recycling Songs

•Sing through several versions of "Rosin the Beau" from Masters #5 and #6 (TG-54, 55). The political parodies from Master #6 were used in American presidential campaigns between 1840 and the present.

CREATE

•One of the most interesting places where songs are varied today is in radio and TV commercials. Have students collect (video/audiotape or take notes) examples of commercial remakes of old songs, classical melodies, and recent pop songs.

•Break the class into small teams of 2 or 3, and have each team make a commercial that uses either an older folk song or a contemporary song. If possible, either tape record or videotape the final products. Students may find it easier to perform their commercial for a video camera or cassette recorder rather than before a "live" class audience.

RESOURCES

Books

Silber, Irwin. *Songs America Voted By.* Harrisburg, PA: Stackpole Books, 1988.

Recordings

Joan Baez: *Any Day Now.* Vanguard 79306, 79307 [Dylan's songs].*Beatles '67-70.* Capitol 90438.

Beatles '67-70. Capitol 90438.

Bob Dylan: Biograph. Columbia C38830.

Folkways: The Original Vision. Smithsonian Folkways SF40001.

Aretha Franklin: 30 Greatest Hits. Atlantic 81668.

Simon & Garfunkel's Greatest Hits. Columbia 31350.

A Vision Shared: A Tribute to Woody Guthrie and Leadbelly. CBS Records 44034.

African and European Singing Styles in America

The way people sing reflects the way they live. For example—people who live and work together on an equal basis tend to sing easily in a group with no leader. In contrast—people who live and work more individually need a strong leader to pull them together at work or when singing. In this section you will study contrasts in African- and European-American singing styles.

What to Listen for

Words are just one of the many important elements of a song style. Whether a song has many words or very few will determine how that song will be sung. **Many African-American songs use few words with much repetition.** This makes for great group singing. It makes songs easier to remember, and repetition gives power to the message by driving it home. In contrast, **many European-American songs are very wordy with little repetition.** In these traditions, solo singing is more common, words must often be written down to remember them, many words can spell out subtle shades of meaning, and consonants must be carefully enunciated or the words will not be understood.

Can you identify which verses below come from the African- American tradition and which come from the European-American tradition?

1. Oh____ it may be,____
   Oh____ it may be,____
   Oh____ it may be,____
   It may be the last time, I don't know.___

2. Go bring me a bag of your father's gold,
   Likewise your mother's fee,
   And the two best horses out of the stall,
   Where there stand thirty and three.

3. Oh, what can you do in a case like that?
   Oh, what can you do but stamp on your hat
   Or on your brother, on your toothbrush,
   Or anything that's helpless?

4. Sun gonna shine on my back door some day,
   Sun gonna shine on my back door some day,
   Wind gonna rise up and blow my blues away.

Below is a "Style Chart" that shows the basic characteristics of the African- and European-American singing styles. Apply the Style Chart to both old and new song recordings, and determine whether the singing style is basically African-American, European-American, or a mixture of both. Remember that the Style Chart only shows basic tendencies—you will always be able to find exceptions.

THE STYLE CHART

African-American	European-American
few words	many words
relaxed consonants	articulated consonants
group singing	solo singing
buzzy or raspy tone	clear tone
open-throated tone	somewhat nasal tone
syncopated rhythms	on-beat rhythms
3-against-2 meters	one meter
obvious beat	subtle or hidden beat
bending melody notes	straight melodies
much melody sliding	some melody sliding
added words/syllables	regular words

The characteristics given in the Style Chart show the styles of singing derived from African cultures south of the Sahara Desert and European cultures found in northern Europe. Other styles of singing exist in both Africa and Europe—for example, the Moslem styles of northern Africa or the eastern European styles found in Slavic countries.

Many Africans south of the Sahara prefer a "buzzy" tone on their musical instruments and in their voices. They often attach bottle caps or loose pieces of metal to instruments to make a continuous buzzing sound.

LISTEN

✔ Students will identify whether songs have **few words, which are repeated** or **many words with little repetition**, and they will describe what happens as a result of this. (Remind students that the entire spectrum from "much repetition" to "wordy" occurs in both African- and European-American music.)

Looking at Lyrics

•The way we sing tells a lot about the way we live. Students should learn that all music, art, and dance reflects cultural patterns—for instance:

➡ When a society has a high degree of group consensus and most people are living on about the same social level (tribal societies/ teenage groups), musical lyrics and other word forms tend to be **less wordy** and group participation is high.

PERFORM

Take a look at rock lyrics. Discuss with the class other ways in which teens show a common bond with each other such as dress, hair styles, or behavior at concerts.

➡ When a society has many social layers (with leaders whose titles are president, exec. vice president, vice president, or asst. vice president), musical lyrics and other word forms become **very wordy** and group participation declines in favor of an audience listening to a leader.

An easy way to see this dynamic in action is to compare church, synagogue, or other group meeting formats. How is the seating arranged? Is there a program that mandates what will happen? Is the format leader-dominated or oriented toward group participation?

DESCRIBE

•Have students rate the lyrics on Master #9 (TG-58) using the following scale:

① much repetition ② fewer words ③ middle ④ fairly wordy ⑤ wordy

✔ Students will identify musical characteristics from the Style Chart that represent tendencies in African-American and European-American singing. (The Style Chart is based on the research of Alan Lomax reported in *Folk Song Style and Culture*.) Students will apply the Style Chart to different recordings of singing using Master #8 (TG-57) duplicated for in-class student use.

Listening to Style Differences

CREATE

•Take the class through some sample songs using Master #7 (TG-56), duplicated as an overhead transparency. Practice each line on the Style Chart—one at a time. Remember that it will take some time for students to establish their frame of reference. Don't stress the idea of one "right answer."

•Use the Style Chart to spark discussion about current popular and rock music. Students should see that rock is heavily influenced by the tendencies listed on the African-American side of the ledger.

RESOURCES

Books

Lomax, Alan. *Folk Song Style and Culture.*
Washington D.C.: American Association for
the Advancement of Science, 1968.

African-American Contributions to American Music

Musical Instruments

Percussion instruments including **drums** of all sizes, **rattles**, **xylophones**, **marimbas**, and **bells** are widely used in Africa south of the Sahara. Before the Civil War, slaves in the United States were not permitted to use drums for fear that they could be used to signal an uprising. Regardless of this ban on drums, rhythm continued to be an important element in many forms of African-American music. In today's music, the important place of the drum set in jazz, rock, and Latin-American styles is directly due to African influence.

Stringed instruments also are widely played in Africa as accompaniment to singing or in combination with other instruments. The **banjo**, developed in America, was based on an African prototype that had a stick neck stuck through a gourd, turtle shell, or other hollow resonator covered with a stretched animal skin. The **gut-bucket** or washtub bass probably developed from another plucked African instrument called the mosquito drum (a flexible young tree bent over and tied to an animal skin stretched over a hole in the ground). The preference for the plucked, slapped or popped (as opposed to bowed) bass in styles like jazz, rock or Latin-American music shows the African influence on a European stringed instrument.

Musical Styles

African-American **work songs** sung during the 19th century included hollers, axe and hammer songs, railroad track-lining songs, and a wide variety of rhythmic songs sung to make the work seem easier. Sweet Honey in the Rock's version of Leadbelly's "Bring Me L'il' Water, Silvy" is an interesting musical arrangement. Compare it to Leadbelly's original on the *Folkways: The Original Vision* recording. "Take This Hammer" (page 43) is a rock-busting hammer song from the experience of black prisoners during the 1930's Great Depression. Notice the "wah" in the lyrics to indicate the hammer blow.

Spirituals—great songs of faith born out of slavery—represent one of America's important song treasures. Some of the hallmarks of the African-American spiritual style in addition to those from the Style Chart are:

- call and response form
- 2-line interchangeable rhyming lines
- Judgement Day theme
- Old Testament Biblical themes

After the Civil War, African-American colleges such as Fisk University sent their choirs to tour the northern United States and Europe. Groups such as the Fisk Jubilee Singers helped to popularize many of the spirituals that are still widely known today.

In the 1920's a new style of black religious song called **gospel** added a new dimension to the spiritual tradition. The acknowledged leader of the gospel movement was Thomas Dorsey. This new style added instruments such as the piano and (at a later time) the Hammond electric organ. It also featured solo quartets or other special performers. Many of the greatest African-American singers of this century, such as Mahalia Jackson or Aretha Franklin, got their start singing in the local church gospel choir.

In contrast to the group singing of work songs and spirituals, **blues** were solo songs that gave vent to the frustrations and personal troubles of the African-American. Early blues from the Mississippi Delta or Texas—called **country blues**—were sung with guitar accompaniment. These early singers often sang three phrases (AAB) that used twelve measures of music—a form called **12-bar blues**. Leadbelly's song "The Bourgeois Blues" (page 31) is an example of this form. The second stage of the blues style was the 1920's **classic blues** featuring female singers such as Bessie Smith with a small jazz band accompaniment using players such as the great trumpet player Louis Armstrong. When players such as Muddy Waters used electric guitars and instruments such as saxophones during the 1940's and 50's, the style became known as **urban blues** or **rhythm and blues**. Eventually the rhythm and blues style gave birth in 1955 to rock 'n' roll, which featured many songs in the 12-bar blues form. Rock 'n' roll stars such as Elvis, Chuck Berry, or Little Richard, who appears on the *A Vision Shared* video tape, sang many early hit songs in this style during the period from 1955 to 1959.

✔ Students will list the types of musical instruments which came from Africa and describe the influence of African musical instruments and technique on contemporary musical practice.

LISTEN

African-American Musical Instruments

•Study the percussion family of instruments used in contemporary rock, Latin and pop ensembles by tracing them back to their ancestors in Africa. Examples include:

conga drums → from large variety of sophisticated drums of all sizes
Cuban cabaça → from calabash rattle with outer seed netting
cowbell or double bell → from a variety of hand-held bells/gongs
claves → from various types of percussion sticks
xylophone & marimba → from xylophones with gourd resonators

PERFORM

timbales → from pairs of drums played with sticks

Keep in mind that names of African instruments change considerably depending on the country or tribe from which they come.

•Have students trace the history of the American banjo.

•Build a washtub bass, also known as a gutbucket.

✔ Students will sing, study and listen to some of the principal types of African-American musical styles.

DESCRIBE

African-American Musical Styles

•Sing several African-American spirituals (Master #4, TG-53, or songs from Alan Lomax, *Folk Songs of North America*).

•Listen to Aretha Franklin's *Amazing Grace* recording, and focus on her use of melodic variation and embellishment.

•Sing and play some of the 12-bar blues verses from Master #11, TG-60; then compare them to Leadbelly's "Bourgeois Blues" (p. 31) in the Student Text. Have students make up their own verses.

CREATE

•Show how 12-bar blues became the prototype for early rock 'n' roll songs which were popular between 1955 and 1959. Examples: Elvis's "Hound Dog" and Little Richard's "Tutti Frutti" or "Long Tall Sally."

•Play "St. Louis Blues" as recorded by Bessie Smith (*Smithsonian Collection of Classic Jazz*). Map out the form of the piece with the class. Which part of the piece is a 12-bar blues?

RESOURCES

Books

Adzinyah, Abraham Kobena, Dumisani Maraire and Judith Cook Tucker. *Let Your Voice Be Heard!* Danbury, CT: World Music Press, 1988. Book and cassette.

George, Luvenia A. *Teaching the Music of Six Different Cultures.* Danbury, CT: World Music Press, 1988. Book and cassette.

Southern, Eileen. *Black American Music*: A History. New York: W.W. Norton, 1971.

Recordings

Recordings available from World Music Press, P.O. Box 2565, Danbury, CT 06813.

Aretha Franklin: Amazing Grace. Atlantic CS2-906.

Smithsonian Collection of Classic Jazz. Smithsonian Institution P6 11891.

Video Tape

Say Amen, Somebody. United Artists Classics. GTN Productions—Pacific Arts Video.

Around the turn of the century, piano styles such as **ragtime** and early forms of **jazz** developed within African-American communities. These fresh new styles, with their exciting syncopated rhythms, quickly became popular with mixed audiences throughout America and even Europe. In the 1920's when phonograph records became practical and less expensive, many of the early jazz bands and blues performers recorded their music on African-American labels such as Paramount or Okeh. Recordings by African-American performers were known up through the 1940's as **race records**. When a race record became a big hit, a **cover** recording was usually made by a white performer to take advantage of its popularity. The practice of making cover recordings can be seen up through 1950's rock 'n' roll with Elvis' version of Joe Turner's "Shake, Rattle and Roll."

In the 1960's the word **soul** began to replace the term **rhythm and blues** as a name for recordings made by African-Americans. By the 60's many elements of African-American music had been absorbed by white performers.

European-American Contributions to American Music

Musical Instruments

Europeans brought musical instruments such as **fiddles** (violins), **concertinas, guitars, mandolins, zithers**, and **pianos** with them to America. During the 18th and 19th centuries, the fiddle was probably the most portable and practical instrument used in the westward expansion of America. A fiddler who could play a lively dance tune was a welcome member of most communities. The piano became a parlor fixture during the 19th century, and a healthy sheet-music industry sprang up to meet the demand for songs by such composers as Stephen Foster. American guitar companies such as C.F. Martin were established as early as 1840, and the guitar gradually grew to a popularity that matched the piano in its impact on American folk and popular music. In the late 1800's a new American instrument called the **Autoharp** was created from a German zither, and it quickly

became a popular folk instrument that is still used in school music programs. Wind instruments such as the cornet, trumpet, saxophone, clarinet, trombone, and others were quickly incorporated into jazz and other forms of American popular music.

Musical Styles

The **ballad** or story song is one of the most important musical contributions made by European-Americans. Ballads from England, Scotland, Ireland, or France became prototypes for sea, railroad, cowboy, lumberjack, and farmer songs sung from Maine to California. Immigrants moving westward during the 19th century often made up their own versions or parodies of well-known ballads such as "Rosin the Beau," which was discussed on page 7.

A form of white **spiritual** known today as the Sacred Harp spiritual or shape-note hymn came into being during the same period (1800-1860) that gave rise to the African-American spiritual. The different-shaped notes were used as a method of learning how to read music. Perhaps the best known song in this style is "Amazing Grace," written by a repentant slave trader who dedicated the rest of his life to fighting the evils of slavery. In the 1920's **gospel** music was created which often featured quartets or family bands who accompanied themselves on guitars, Autoharps, fiddles, or **string band** instruments.

Fiddle tunes such as reels and jigs were a staple of life in 19th century America. Tunes such as "Turkey in the Straw" or "Arkansas Traveler" were played for dances and eventually used in stage productions such as the minstrel show. Today these same fiddle tunes are still part of a branch of country music called **bluegrass**, which features fiddle, guitar, mandolin, and the five-string banjo—an instrument that crossed over from African-American music.

In the 1920's when phonograph records became practical and radios found a place in most American homes, a new style of European-American music was born. Record promoters went into Appalachia and the Southwest to find new recording talent. The new style was dubbed **hillbilly**, and the name stuck for about twenty-five years. The southeastern Appalachian style followed the lead of the Carter

LISTEN

✔ Students will learn about the development of **phonograph recordings** and the role played by African-American musicians in American culture.

From "Race" Records to "Soul" CDs

•Discuss the history of phonograph recordings:

1877 - Thomas Edison invented phonograph (tinfoil, then wax cylinder)

1887 - Emile Berliner patented flat disk instead of cylinder

1906 - development of electrical (rather than mechanical) recording

1920s - quality of disk recording became practical; new African-American labels such as *Okeh* or *Paramount* made recordings known as **race records**. Hit recordings by African Americans were quickly **covered** by European Americans on other labels. **Jukeboxes** became common.

PERFORM

1946 - reel-to-reel tape recording

1948 - unbreakable vinyl plastic 33⅓ RPM records (LPs)

1949 - Billboard Magazine reclassified race records as **rhythm & blues**

1960s - cassettes developed; the term **soul** began to replace **rhythm and blues (R&B)** as a label for African-American recordings

1980s - digital recording and CDs

DESCRIBE

✔ Students will list the types of musical instruments which came from Europe and describe how they became part of American folk and popular music.

European-American Musical Instruments

•List the folk and popular musical styles and types of ensembles in which these instruments (and others listed in the Student Text) are used:

piano → rock, country, blues, jazz, gospel, soul, etc.
guitar → rock, country, blues, folk, bluegrass, jazz, reggae, etc.
violin (fiddle) → country, bluegrass, folk, rock, jazz, cajun, etc.

CREATE

•Study the interesting history of the European string bass—how its playing technique has been affected by African Americans and how it has changed.

➡ Rhythmic slapping, plucking and hitting of strings in jazz style
➡ Change to electric bass (bass guitar)—hitting strings with thumb

•Compare members of the zither family (strings stretched across a board) including the piano, Autoharp, zither, mountain (Appalachian) dulcimer, and the hammered dulcimer. Listen to recordings and discuss playing technique.

•Show how European instruments such as the trumpet and the saxophone have been used in different ways in various types of ensembles.

RESOURCES

Books

The New Grove Dictionary of Musical Instruments.
    3 vols. New York: Macmillan, 1984.

Family, and family bands sprang up often featuring duets by brothers or sisters. The southwestern region followed the lead of Jimmie Rodgers and developed a Texas cowboy style as sung by the famous movie cowboys Gene Autry and Roy Rogers. As the 1930's turned to the '40's, the name hillbilly gradually gave way to the term **country and western** (which showed the original southeastern and southwestern roots). Performers from both styles were featured on radio shows such as Nashville's *Grand Ole Opry* and Chicago's *National Barn Dance*. After World War II, the country and western style gradually incorporated electric instruments, a drum set, and in the late '60's—some elements of the rock style. Eventually the term **country** was used to describe this new style of music.

Elvis Presley, star of '50's rock 'n' roll, showed an interesting combination of style influences. In addition to the African-American rhythm and blues discussed earlier, he was also much influenced by European-American hillbilly and gospel styles. Before he became a rock 'n' roll star, he had sung the country and western song "Old Shep" on Nashville's Grand Ole Opry.

Perhaps the most important musical element that came from Europe is **harmony**—the functional use of chords—sometimes called the "vertical" element in music. Listen to church hymns or chords on a guitar to hear good examples of harmony at work.

In the 20th century, American popular music absorbed both African- and European-American styles in a variety of different mixtures. On the stage, the minstrel show gave way to vaudeville, revues, and finally the Broadway musical. Ragtime and blues were incorporated into jazz in its many forms—dixieland, boogie woogie, swing, bebop, and many more. Rhythm and blues (R&B) and country and western (C&W) combined to form rock 'n' roll and the many varieties of rock with prefixes like hard (rock), psychedelic, punk, country, and heavy metal. Almost all American popular music today is a fusion of elements from African and European musical influences. It will be interesting to see how American music absorbs styles from other parts of the world in the global village of the 1990's.

Unit Review

REVIEW QUESTIONS

1. What is the oral tradition, and how does music change as a result of it?

2. How can popular sheet music turn into folk music? Can you give examples of songs where this has happened?

3. How many of the singing style characteristics can you remember from the Style Chart on page 8? Divide a blank page into two columns headed by African- American and European-American; then list as many style characteristics as you can remember. Check your work.

4. What contributions have African-Americans made to American popular music? Instruments? Types of music?

5. What contributions have European-Americans made to American popular music? Instruments? Types of music?

VOCABULARY DISCUSSION

1. Discuss how **race records** were often **covered** by white performers.

2. How do popular singers and instrumentalists use the **variation** idea to make their music more interesting? Find recordings to illustrate your points.

3. What are two different meanings for the label **rhythm and blues**?

4. How was the **country & western** style a mixture of several regional types of music?

5. Do we still have **work songs** today?

CREATIVE PROJECTS

• Write new words to a well-known tune.

• Apply the Style Chart (page 8) to some of your favorite songs.

• Make a gutbucket and form a jug band with washboard, guitars, and kazoos.

• Select one of the songs in the back of the book and see if you can perform it in different styles such as C&W or R&B.

LISTEN

✔ Students will learn how the European-American sacred harp **spirituals** differ from African-American spirituals.

Amazing Grace . . . "how varied the sound"

•Study and sing through Master #3 (TG-52) "Amazing Grace." Contrast it with "Wade in the Water" from Master #4 (TG-53).

•Explain that "Amazing Grace" was written by the repentant English captain of a slave ship who quit the slave trade and dedicated his life to overcoming its evils. Watch the *Amazing Grace with Bill Moyers* video tape.

•Play several different recordings of "Amazing Grace" by Aretha Franklin, Judy Collins, Sacred Harp singers, etc.

PERFORM

•How does the music and each of the performances stack up against the Style Charts on Masters #7 and #8 (TG-56,57)?

•Show students how the original Sacred Harp spirituals used shaped notes (Master #3, TG-52) to teach people how to read music, and point out that these songs are still sung in that tradition throughout the South by beginning with the syllables fa-so-la.

◇   ◁   ○   ☐
Mi   Fa   Sol   La

Students may ask how it is possible to sing all eight notes of a diatonic scale without *do, re or ti*. Have them discover how the tetrachord *mi fa sol la* repeats itself with the same half- and whole-steps in the tones *ti do re mi*.

DESCRIBE

•Ask them to find songs that use the tetrachord *ti do re mi*. Examples include "Londonderry Air" and "Lift Every Voice."

✔ Students will make historical connections from 1930s hillbilly musical styles to rock performers of the '50s through the '90s.

Dynamic Duos

•Listen to some of the brothers and sisters duet acts from 1930s hillbilly music on *The Smithsonian Collection of Classic Country Music*, Side 4. Particularly good examples are the Monroe Brothers (Bill Monroe went on to become the "Founder of Bluegrass") and the Blue Sky Boys.

CREATE

•This basic vocal duet sound (based on parallel 3rds) was reworked in the 1950s by the Everly Brothers and by Buddy Holly and the Crickets; in the 1960s it was used by Simon and Garfunkel and by the Beatles.

✔ **Assessment**

•Use Masters #12 and #13 (TG-61-62) to assess students' understanding of Unit One. Other assessment should include performance and projects.

RESOURCES

Books

Original Sacred Harp. Bremen, GA: Sacred Harp Publishing Company, 1971.

Recordings

Colors of the Day: The Best of Judy Collins. Elecktra 75030.

Aretha Franklin: Amazing Grace. Atlantic CS2-906.

Old Harp Singing. Folkways 2356. [Sacred Harp]

The Smithsonian Collection of Classic Country Music. Smithsonian Institution P8 15640.

Most recordings available from Elderly Instruments, 1100 N. Washington, P.O. Box 14210, Lansing, MI 48901. Write for catalog.

Video Tape

Amazing Grace with Bill Moyers. PBS Home Video.

Woody Guthrie

He really believed in the power of music to make people alive.
—Millard Lampell, Almanac Singers

LEARNING OBJECTIVES

After reading UNIT TWO and doing the
activities you will be able to:

- Describe the Dust Bowl and Great Depression
of the 1930s and tell how Woody Guthrie was
both a product and a shaper of those times.
- List contributions Woody Guthrie made to
American music.
- Identify other musicians associated with and
influenced by him.
- Describe Guthrie's musical style, his roots in
hillbilly music, and his influence on the Folk
Revival of the 1950s and '60s folk-rock .

WOODY'S SONGS

In UNIT TWO you will learn about the life
and music of Woody Guthrie, an American
original. The video tape *A Vision Shared* tes-
tifies to the power of his influence on generations of singers and songwriters. He became
the model for guitar-playing folksingers who
sing their original songs rooted in the folk tradition—songs about social justice, the environment, the down and out, the right to a decent
job with honest pay, or the American dream.

What you will also find here is the portrait of
a man whose life speaks to the major issues for
our day. Woody was a citizen of the world who
went far beyond the nationalistic values of his
time. He was also completely at home with
people of all races and colors. So take this opportunity to learn from his music and his life.

*Woody is just Woody. Thousands of people
do not know he had any other name. He is
just a voice and a guitar. He sings the songs
of a people and I suspect that he is, in a way,
that people. Harsh voiced and nasal, his
guitar hanging like a tire iron on a rusty rim,
there is nothing sweet about Woody, and
there is nothing sweet about the songs he
sings. But there is something more
important for those who will listen. There is
the will of a people to endure and fight
against oppression. I think we call this the
American spirit.*

—John Steinbeck

In Unit Two, students will learn about the life and music of Woody Guthrie. The material covered in this unit will make much more sense to students if they have some way of personalizing it, so try one or more of the stategies below.

LISTEN

Oral Histories of the Great Depression and World War II

•Have your students find a relative or neighbor who lived through the 1930s and '40s, and have them collect oral histories of the period. Here are some possible questions they could ask.

How much did things (such as candy or ice cream cones) cost in those days? How much did people earn per hour for jobs?

What did you do for entertainment?

PERFORM

What was school like in those days?

Were lots of people out of work? Did the Dust Bowl affect this area?

Did hobos ever come to the door asking for handouts?

How did people feel about President F.D. Roosevelt and his programs?

When did electricity come to rural areas in this part of the country?

What new inventions changed your life?

What songs or musical activities did you do? Did you go to dances?

DESCRIBE

What kind of musical groups played for the dances?

How did World War II change things?

You will want to coach students on proper interview behavior. Interviews could be taped or notes could be written by the interviewer. Have students bring their results to class and use them to create a backdrop for the story of Woody Guthrie's life and songs.

Themes to Explore

CREATE

•Find out more about some of the themes Woody fought for and wrote about—

Migrant workers

The union movement (IWW, CIO, AFL, UMW, etc.)

Homeless people

Unemployment

Peace

RESOURCES

Books

Lomax, Alan, Woody Guthrie and Pete Seeger. *Hard Hitting Songs for Hard-Hit People.* New York: Music Sales, 1967.

Seeger, Pete and Bob Reiser. *Carry It On.* New York: Simon and Schuster, 1985 [songs of the labor movement].

Seeger, Pete and Bob Reiser. *Everybody Says Freedom.* New York: W.W. Norton, 1989.

Sing Out! Magazine. P.O. Box 5253, Bethlehem, PA 18015-5253, has been publishing great songs and information on folk music since 1950. They also publish a good book of lyrics and chords to over 1200 folk and pop song called *Rise Up Singing*.

Woody's Life

The Early Days

Woodrow Wilson Guthrie was born July 14, 1912 in Okemah, Oklahoma. Woody had this to say about his home town:

> Okemah, Oklahoma, where I come from was one of the singingest, square-dancingest, drinkingest, preachingest, walkingest, talkingest, laughingest, cryingest, shootingest, fistfightingest, bleedingest, gamblingest, gun, club and razor carryingest of our ranch and farm towns, because it blossomed into one of our first Oil Boom Towns.

By age 14, his mother was institutionalized with what was later diagnosed as Huntington's chorea, his father was crippled and out of money, and his sister Clara was killed in a fire. Woody and his older brother Roy were left to watch after themselves. So he left town and travelled to Houston, Texas and the Gulf . . .

> doing all kind of odd jobs, hoeing figs, orchards, pickin' grapes, hauling wood, helping carpenters and cement men, working with water well drillers. I carried my harmonica and played in barber shops, at [shoe] shine stands, in front of shows, around the pool halls, . . . sang and played with Negroes, Indians, whites, farmers, town folks, truck drivers, and with every kind of singers you can think of. I learned all the tricks of strings and music and all of the songs that I could remember and learn by ear.

He returned to the Texas panhandle town of Pampa for a few years where he played in a hillbilly band, worked at odd jobs, married Mary Jennings and had two children. Woody also worked as a local musician along with his dad's half-brother Jeff.

> Jeff . . . taught me how to chord on the guitar. After a while I was rattling around with him playing my way at the ranch and farm house dances. We worked our way up to playing inside of the city limits, and then for the banquet thrown by the Chamber of Commerce. We played for rodeos, centennials, carnivals, parades, fairs, just bustdown parties, and played several nights and days a week just to hear our own boards rattle and our strings roar around in the wind. It was along in these days I commenced singing, I guess it was singing.

The Dust Bowl

In 1929 the New York Stock Market crashed signaling the beginning of a Great Depression that would last well into the 1940s and World War II. During the 1930s, great dust storms followed on the heels of drought and blew away the topsoil on many of the Great Plains states such as Oklahoma. Farmers lost their homes and land, banks went bankrupt (there was no FDIC then), and many people were out of work.

Woody, like many others, took to the road in search of food, shelter, and a job to support his family. He headed for California and found work as a sign painter and musician.

> I hit the highway to look around for a place for us to go. I carried my pockets full of paint brushes and my guitar slung across my back. I painted all kinds of window signs, posters, show cards, banners, car and truck signs, in the daylight and played with my hat down on the old saloon floor after night had set in. Got to California and went up and down the west coast a few times, found a cousin of mine, Jack, and we took a fifteen minute radio program in order to collect us enough prestige around at the saloons to ask for a two dollar guarantee for six hours.

His songs **"I Ain't Got No Home"** (p. 39), **"Going Down the Road"** (p. 35), **"Do Re Mi"** (p. 34), **"Deportee"** (p. 33), and **"Vigilante Man"** (p. 46) describe in music what the novelist John Steinbeck wrote about in *Grapes of Wrath* or Dorothea Lange treated in her photographs. He got a job singing his songs on radio station KFVD and wrote a regular newspaper column for the *People's Daily World*.

✔ Students will sing songs about the loss of a home, the loss of a parent or the difficulties in the life of a wanderer. They will discuss these themes and how their lives or the lives of people they know may be affected.

LISTEN

Homeless

•The number of homeless people in the United States and the rest of the world makes Woody's song **"I Ain't Got No Home"** very contemporary. Don't shy away from tough subjects like this one—music is one of the best ways of dealing with this issue.

•Watch the *A Vision Shared* video tape; listen to *The Original Vision*; then sing "I Ain't Got No Home" from the Student Text (p. 39) with instruments such as guitars or Autoharps.

PERFORM

•You may wish to sing and listen to some other songs that deal with this same theme:

"Streets of London" by Ralph McTell in *Folk Festival*

"Hard Times Come Again No More" by Stephen Foster in *Stephen Foster Songbook.*

"Aragon Mill" by Si Kahn in *New Folk Favorites*

"Homeless" from Paul Simon's *Graceland* album

DESCRIBE

The Farm Aid concerts of the late '80s contained many songs on this same topic.

Songs from the book *Hard Hitting Songs for Hard-Hit People* include "The Boll Weevil" (p. 30), "The Farmer Is the Man" (p. 32), "Down and Out" (p. 50) and "Wanderin' " (p. 66).

Songs from John McCutcheon's songbook *Water From Another Time* include "Gone Gonna Rise Again" (p. 22), "The Farmer Is the Woman" (p. 16), "Dearest Martha" (p. 18) and "Room Here for Another" (p. 58).

CREATE

•Sing and play **"Going Down the Road"** (Student Text, p. 35) and share some of the photos by people like Dorothea Lange in the book *Hard Hitting Songs for Hard-Hit People*. Ask students to make up new one-line verses to the song.

•Another song from the African-American tradition that gets right to the feeling level is "Sometimes I Feel Like a Motherless Child." This song is also an easy song for which students can create new verses.

•Draw students into a discussion of whether homeless people live in your community or nearby communities. Ask them to brainstorm some possible solutions to the problem.

RESOURCES

Books

Schmid, Will. *Folk Festival.* Milwaukee: Hal Leonard, 1979.

McCutcheon, John. *Water From Another Time.* Milwaukee: Hal Leonard, 1989.

Schmid, Will, ed. *New Folk Favorites.* Milwaukee: Hal Leonard, 1987 [45 songs by contemporary singer/songwriters].

Stephen Foster Songbook. New York: Dover, 1974.

Recordings

Paul Simon: Graceland. Warner Bros. WB 25447-4.

I saw the hundreds of thousands of stranded, broke, hungry, idle, miserable people that lined the highways all out through the leaves and the underbrush. I heard these people sing in their jungle [hobo] camps and in their Federal Work Camps and sang songs I made up for them over the air waves.

When Woody's radio job produced enough income, his younger brother George joined him in California. Shortly thereafter, he bought a house and sent for Mary and the two girls. Later, they had a son, Bill Rogers Guthrie, named after the famous humorist Will Rogers and an actor friend Will Geer.

Throughout his life Woody often got the wanderlust. The songs **"Hard Travelin'"** (p. 37), **"Ramblin' 'Round"** (p. 47) and **"Hobo's Lullaby"** (p. 38) tell about his travels during the 1930s. He took the family back to Oklahoma, borrowed $35 from his brother Roy and headed off to New York City where he stayed with actor Will Geer and his wife. During this period he met **Alan Lomax**, who with his father John had recorded American folk songs for the Library of Congress. In March of 1940, Lomax invited Guthrie down to Washington D.C. where he interviewed him and recorded his songs. It was during this same period that Woody met **Pete Seeger**, whom he described as "a long tall string bean kid from up in New England." Together with Alan Lomax they collaborated on a landmark book entitled *Hard Hitting Songs for Hard-Hit People* (published over twenty-five years later), which along with the twelve *Dust Bowl Ballads* recorded for Victor serve as a first-rate documentary history of the period.

Guthrie's strong support of organized labor took him and Pete Seeger on the road singing songs for the movement. **"Union Maid"** (p. 45) was composed during this trip. Guthrie became a mentor for Pete Seeger, who returned the favor years later by teaching Guthrie's songs to several new generations of singers. During this trip, Guthrie and Seeger stopped off in Tennessee at the Highlander Center, a leadership training camp for the Labor Movement and later the Civil Rights Movement.

When Woody got back to New York City he became increasingly popular and successful as a radio singer on shows such as the *Pursuit of Happiness* and *Cavalcade of America* (In the 1940s, music on the radio was live, not recorded.). While this success brought in more money than he had ever made, it forced him to sing songs and commercials that he didn't like.

I got disgusted with the whole sissified and nervous rules of censorship on all of my songs and ballads, and drove off down the road across the southern states again.

World War II and Beyond

Roosevelt's New Deal had put people back to work rebuilding America. Like Guthrie, artists such as **Thomas Hart Benton** (painting), **Martha Graham** (dance), or **John Steinbeck** (literature) were recording the American experience. While in California, Guthrie was contracted to write songs for the Bonneville Power Administration to promote the Grand Coulee and Bonneville dams. The song **"Roll On, Columbia"** (p. 47) was written for this purpose.

When Woody returned to New York City, he joined Pete Seeger and the **Almanac Singers** who gave Sunday afternoon concerts called **"hootenannies"** in the basement of their Greenwich Village house and other places. When America entered World War II after Pearl Harbor, Woody joined the Merchant Marine and shipped out with **Cisco Houston**, a singer/guitarist with whom he would eventually make a series of records for Moe Asch and Folkways Records. Other musical associates included the **Weavers, Josh White, Leadbelly** and **Sonny Terry**. Woody's best known song **"This Land Is Your Land"** (p. 44) was written during this period as a response to a World War II favorite "God Bless America."

Woody was divorced and remarried twice, and had other children including **Arlo** who appears on the *A Vision Shared* video tape. Woody spent the last eleven years of his life in hospitals suffering from Huntington's chorea and died on October 3, 1967 in New York City.

✔ Students will learn about the '30s **Dust Bowl** and its impact on the Depression.

Dust Bowl Refugees

LISTEN

•Watch the video tape; then sing and play Guthrie's songs **"Do Re Mi"** (Student Text, p. 34), **"Deportee"** (p. 33) and **"Vigilante Man"** (p. 46).

•You may wish to have students read or watch parts of a video tape of the movie version of Steinbeck's *Grapes of Wrath*.

•The song "Deportee" raises interesting possibilities for branching into music and discussion of Mexican-American culture.

•Compare the effects of the Dust Bowl to some of the aftermath of the Mount St. Helens volcano. Some effects (in both cases) were that the dust clogged car motors and blew in large dust clouds across the country.

PERFORM

•Sing and play the songs **"Hard Travelin' "** (Student Text, p. 37), **"Ramblin' 'Round"** (p. 47) and **"Hobo's Lullaby"** (p. 38); then discuss life "on the road" for hobos including the so-called "jungle camp" or hobo city. Hobos did not consider themselves "bums," but rather men of the road who did not choose to work a steady job in any one place. Other songs you might wish to sing are "Hallelujah, I'm a Bum" or Tom Paxton's "Ramblin' Boy." Do hobos still "ride the rods" (hitch rides on trains) today?

✔ Students will learn about the role that radio played in the 20th century.

DESCRIBE

Radio From Wireless to Walkman

•A brief history of radio

1887 - Heinrich Hertz invents spark generator and receiver

1901 - Guglielmo Marconi transmits radio signal across the Atlantic

1920s - crystal radio sets with earphones

1930s - electrical vacuum-tube radios featuring live music (not records)

1948 - transistor invented, leading to miniature portable radios

CREATE

1950s - gradual move to disc jockeys playing records

•Live radio performances like the *Grand Ole Opry* or the *National Barn Dance* during the 1930s and '40s boosted the careers of many performers like Woody Guthrie. In the 1950s that function would gradually shift to television, where performers like Elvis Presley or the Beatles were introduced to the mass audience on programs like the *Ed Sullivan Show*.

•During the Great Depression and World War II, the radio became the new "hearth" around which the family gathered to hear FDR's *Fireside Chats*, news of the war or to enjoy radio entertainment. Discuss with students whether this role is now played by TV.

RESOURCES

Books

Old Time Stringband Songbook. New York: Music Sales, 1964 [full of good Depression songs— originally published as *New Lost City Ramblers Songbook*].

Recordings

New Lost City Ramblers: Songs From the Depression. Folkways 5264.

The Very Best of Tom Paxton. Flying Fish 519.

Woody's Music

Woody Guthrie's musical life is a testament to the notion that making music is as natural as breathing or eating. He drew his inspiration and power from the people.

The worst thing that can happen to you is to cut yourself loose from the people. And the best thing is to sort of vaccinate yourself right into the big streams and blood of the people.

> *I CANNOT HELP BUT LEARN MY MOST*
> *FROM YOU WHO COUNT YOURSELF LEAST*
> *AND CANNOT HELP BUT FEEL MY BEST WHEN*
> *YOU THAT NEED ME MOST ASK ME TO HELP*
> *YOU AND I NEVER DID KNOW*
> *EXACTLY WHY THIS WAS*
> *THAT IS JUST THE WAY WE ARE BUILT*
>
> —*Woody Guthrie*

He loved to sing and he believed in the power of music to help make things better.

Oh I love to hear houses sing, I love to hear windows yell. I remember livin' in the hope that when I got out of those old pesky Army camps, I'd hear every door and every window, just for one night, sing all night long,'til a new day cracked. I ask ya Mr. President, please, let everybody everywhere, for just one night, sing all night long: Love songs, work songs, new hope songs. That would cure every soul in our jails and asylums, and most of the sick in our hospitals.

He believed that music was for everybody, not just a select group, and he believed that anyone could make his or her own songs.

You know you are as good a songwriter as there is, but you might not believe it. If you don't believe it, that's why you're not. All you have to do is sit down and write up what's wrong and how to fix it. That's all there is to it.

He lived a life that recognized the values of men and women of all races, colors and creeds. The following quote comes out of the series of recordings he made for Folkways Records with Cisco Houston and Sonny Terry (harmonica).

I talked to Sonny about these things in his art and he tells me that he is blind and that he still knows that his people can see a world where we all vote, eat, work, talk, plan and think together and with all of our spokes and wheels rolling and all of our selves well dressed and well housed and well fed. These are the things that the artist in Blind Sonny Terry knows and sees in his blindness. These are the upland echoes of the things that stir and sing along his big muddies. These are the plans and visions seen in the kiss and whisper of tall tree jack pines falling into the chutes to make your papery pulps. These are the freedoms. These are the samples of the kinds of soul art that the Negro, Indian, Mexican, the Irish, the Jew, the Russian, the Greek, Italian, all of us, have to bring to be seen and heard.

Woody's music reflected the hillbilly singing and instrumental style. He was extremely prolific and wrote almost every day. Mill Lampell said this in *A Tribute to Woody Guthrie*:

Woody's guitar playing wasn't much. Sort of casual, down-home, Carter Family style with some Jimmie Rodgers licks thrown in. He blew some free-wheeling mouth harp. Played pretty fair mandolin. And a wild fiddle, holding it tucked under his ribs the country way. In a pinch, he could also get some clackety music out of a couple of soup spoons.

Woody performed about the same way he drove. As though his brakes were shot and he wasn't too sure what was coming next. His playing was peppered with sharps, flats, hit and misses, and several notes never before heard on land, sea or air. But it was harsh and honest, exploding with life.

Nobody knows just how many songs Woody made up. A collector claims to have counted over a thousand. But that would only be the ones Woody took the trouble to write down. It wouldn't include the songs that slipped away in the dusty wind, the ones that vanished in the clank and rattle of a fast freight crossing through the hills in the darkness.

Following are some of Woody's best known songs for which he used existing melodies.

"Union Maid" from "Redwing"

"Sinking of the Reuben James" from "Wildwood Flower"

"This Land Is Your Land" from "Little Darlin' Pal of Mine"

"Tom Joad" from "John Hardy"

"Jesus Christ" from "Jesse James"

"The Philadelphia Lawyer" from "The Jealous Lover"

"Pastures of Plenty" from "Pretty Polly"

"Roll On, Columbia" and "Ramblin' 'Round" from "Goodnight Irene"

LISTEN

✔ Students will experience some of the patriotic feeling of World War II and learn how Americans worked and sang together to win the war. They will contrast this with some of the anti-war songs and feelings that came out of the Viet Nam War.

This Land Is Your Land

• Some of the great music of World War II:

– Irving Berlin's "God Bless America" was often sung by Kate Smith. Make a connection to "The Battle Hymn of the Republic" which was composed for a similar purpose during the Civil War.

– Woody Guthrie's "This Land Is Your Land" was his answer to "God Bless America." Was Woody trying to paint a different picture of America? How many of the verses have students sung before?

PERFORM

– You might wish to sing or listen to songs such as "Don't Sit Under the Apple Tree" or "I'll Be Home for Christmas." Two musicals which deal with some aspects of the war are *South Pacific* and *White Christmas*.

– Listen to some big band music of Glenn Miller or Count Basie.

• Ask students to interview their grandparents about war efforts such as victory gardens, war bonds, rationing, women in the work force ("Rosy the Riveter"), gradual integration of blacks and whites in the armed forces, etc.

DESCRIBE

• Sing or listen to anti-war songs from the '60s such as Bob Dylan's "With God On Our Side" or "Blowin' In the Wind," Simon & Garfunkel's "7 O'Clock News," Pete Seeger's "Where Have All the Flowers Gone?" or Country Joe and the Fish's "Fixin' to Die Rag." A movie such as *Born on the 4th of July* addresses this same theme. Contrast these songs with WWII songs.

✔ Students will compare some of Woody's songs with the original melodies on which they were based.

Something Borrowed

CREATE

• Review the new words to an old tune idea from Unit One; then sing and play Leadbelly's **"Goodnight Irene"** (p. 36) and Woody's new versions of it— **"Roll On, Columbia"** and **"Ramblin' 'Round"** (p. 47). Have students compose new verses to "Ramblin' 'Round." Sing other songs from the list, p.16.

• The song **"Union Maid"** (p. 45) uses the melody of the fiddle dance tune "Redwing." Sing or listen to other songs of the union movement including "Solidarity Forever," "Which Side Are You On?" or Joe Hill's parody "Pie in the Sky" from *Carry It On*. Interesting newer union commentaries on the closing of American factories come in Larry Penn's song "Nobody Cares About That" or Si Kahn's song "Aragon Mill" from *New Folk Favorites*.

RESOURCES

Books

Lomax, Alan. *Folksongs of North America in the English Language.* New York: Doubleday, 1960 [the most extensive and best overall collection of American folk music].

Schmid, Will, ed. *New Folk Favorites.* Milwaukee: Hal Leonard, 1987.

Seeger, Pete and Bob Reiser . *Carry It On.* New York: Simon and Schuster, 1985 [songs of the labor movement].

Recordings

Pete Seeger, Jane Sapp, & Si Kahn: *Carry It On: Songs of America's Working People.* Flying Fish 104.

Woody's Influence

Woody Guthrie set the mold for generations of singers and songwriters. Foremost among his musical associates was **Pete Seeger,** dean of the American folk movement since 1950. After touring and singing with Guthrie throughout the 1940s, Seeger formed a new group called the **Weavers** and the **Folk Revival** of the 1950s was born. The movie *Wasn't That A Time!* reviews this period when **coffee houses** were the place to hear folk music, poetry and social commentary, and singer/guitar players gathered in living rooms for **hootenannies** [group sings]. Other Folk Revival groups that followed the Weavers' success were the **Kingston Trio,** the **Brothers Four,** the **Limelighters,** the **Chad Mitchell Trio,** and **Peter, Paul, and Mary.** Solo folksingers included **Joan Baez, Tom Paxton, Odetta, Judy Collins,** and **Ramblin' Jack Elliott.** All of these artists recorded Woody's songs.

In 1960, a young fellow by the name of Robert Zimmerman attended the University of Minnesota, changed his name to **Bob Dylan,** and dedicated his life to becoming the next Woody Guthrie. Dylan read and quoted Guthrie from his autobiography *Bound for Glory* or from *Sing Out!* Magazine, dressed like Guthrie, listened to all his records, sang, and played guitar and harmonica in the Guthrie style. Bob Dylan made a pilgrimage to New York City to visit Woody in the hospital and was so elated after seeing him that he exclaimed . . .

> I know Woody . . . I know him and met him and saw him and sang to him. I know Woody!

Dylan met Seeger and others in the New York folk community and was soon a rising star in the Greenwich Village coffeehouses. Dylan's "Song to Woody" is an homage to his mentor set to the tune of Guthrie's "1913 Massacre."

In 1965, Dylan and others such as the **Byrds** created an interesting blend of **folk-rock.** Others who recorded Guthrie songs at this time included **Country Joe and the Fish, Jesse Colin Young** and **Ry Cooder.** At the time of Woody Guthrie's death in 1967, the nation's young had heeded his clarion call for change and were challenging the establishment at every turn.

Unit Review

REVIEW QUESTIONS

1. How do the songs "I Ain't Got No Home," "Going Down the Road," "Do Re Mi," "Deportee" and "Vigilante Man" reflect Guthrie's dust bowl and California experiences?

2. Who were the early influences on Woody's musical style? What instruments did he play?

3. How does the song, "This Land Is Your Land" compare to other patriotic American songs such as "God Bless America" or "America the Beautiful"?

4. Who were some of the musicians influenced by Woody Guthrie?

5. During the 1950s McCarthy era, Guthrie was accused of being "un-American." Why do you think he was so controversial? What would Woody sing about if he were alive today?

MORE ABOUT WOODY GUTHRIE

If you would like to read more about Woody and hear more of his music, try these:

Guthrie, Woody. *Bound for Glory.* New York: Dutton, 1943.   —his autobiography

Hard Travelin': Woody Guthrie. (MGM/UA release 600884). —70-min. video

Klein, Joe. *Woody Guthrie: A Life.* New York: Knopf, 1980.

Lomax, Alan, Woody Guthrie and Pete Seeger. *Hard Hitting Songs for Hard-Hit People.* New York: Music Sales, 1967.

The Woody Guthrie Songbook. New York: Woody Guthrie Publications, 1976.

Recordings —see listing of other Guthrie recordings on liner notes to *Folkways: The Original Vision.* Smithsonian Folkways.

CREATIVE PROJECTS

• Try to find a way to see Jeff Waxman's play, *Woody Guthrie's American Song,* and/or make your own musical play about Woody (idea— What if Woody were to come back for a visit?).

• Take Woody's advice and make a list of some things that "need fixin'"; then make a song, poem, rap, drawing, poster, etc. about the most important ideas on the list.

LISTEN

✔ Students will sing, play or listen to music by some of the musicians influenced by Woody Guthrie.

Woody's Legacy

•Sing, play or listen to songs by the following:

Pete Seeger

"Where Have All the Flowers Gone?" "If I Had a Hammer," "Turn, Turn, Turn"

Bob Dylan

"Blowin' In the Wind," "The Times They Are A-Changing," "Mr. Tambourine Man," "Don't Think Twice" or "Hard Rain's Gonna Fall"

PERFORM

Joan Baez

"Diamonds & Rust," or "The Night They Drove Old Dixie Down"

Tom Paxton

"Peace Will Come," "Where I'm Bound" or "Ramblin' Boy" from *Ramblin Boy*

Larry Long and children of Oklahoma

It Takes a Lot of People [Tribute to Woody Guthrie]

DESCRIBE

•Study the impact of Woody Guthrie on the performers on the *A Vision Shared* video tape and recording.

Discuss the comments of Bruce Springsteen, U2, Bob Dylan and others.

Listen to stylistic differences from the recordings *The Original Vision* and *A Vision Shared*. How do they compare with the way the students are singing the songs from the Student Text?

✔ Students will study the rise of the style known as folk rock.

Folk Rock—From Acoustic to Electric

CREATE

•Listen to the 1965 Byrds' recordings of Seeger's song "Turn, Turn, Turn" and Dylan's song "Mr. Tambourine Man." Listen to Simon & Garfunkel and Dylan recordings from this same period.

•Ask students to identify singer/songwriters who are doing folk or acoustic rock today. Listen to singers such as Tracy Chapman.

✔ **Assessment**

•Use Master #14 (TG-63) to help assess students' understanding of Unit Two (and Three). Other assessment vehicles might include performance, composition projects, listening analysis, essays or research reports.

RESOURCES

Recordings

Tracy Chapman. Elektra 75030.

The Byrds: Greatest Hits. Columbia 9516.

Joan Baez: Greatest Hits and Others. Vanguard 79332.

The Very Best of Tom Paxton. Flying Fish 519.

Bob Dylan: Biograph. Columbia C38830.

The Essential Pete Seeger. Vanguard 97/98.

Larry Long and children of Oklahoma: It Takes a Lot of People. Flying Fish 508 [Tribute to Woody Guthrie].

Leadbelly

The King of the 12-string Guitar

LEARNING OBJECTIVES

After reading UNIT THREE and doing the activities you will be able to:

• Describe how Leadbelly's music reflects or differs from the experience of African Americans living in the United States from 1900 until 1950.

• List contributions Huddie Ledbetter made to American music.

• Identify other musicians associated with and influenced by him.

• Describe Leadbelly's musical style and his musical roots in field hollers, dance tunes, spirituals, blues, prison songs and ballads.

• Sing and/or play some of Leadbelly's songs.

LEADBELLY'S SONGS

U NIT THREE explores the life and music of Huddie Ledbetter, better known as Leadbelly. Leadbelly was one of the last of the country blues guitar players who brought us both a glimpse of the past and a look into the future where African-American music would have a dominant influence on the rise of rock 'n' roll and other musical styles. Through his recordings at the Library of Congress and Folkways Records, Leadbelly enriched our knowledge of African-American music and culture.

The life of Leadbelly is a story of both triumph and tragedy. The tragedy is that he, like other members of his race, was subjected to discrimination, economic hardship and violence. The triumph is that he was able to overcome many of these conditions and become one of the most significant figures in 20th century American folk and popular music.

LADY: *What's the matter with your guitar? What's all this writing on it?*

VAL: *Autographs of famous musicians. See this name here. Leadbelly?*

LADY: *Leadbelly?*

VAL: *Greatest man ever lived on the twelve-string guitar! Played it so good he broke the stone heart of a Texas Governor and won himself a pardon out of jail.*

—Tennessee Williams
from the play **Orpheus Descending**

In Unit Three, students will learn about the life and music of Leadbelly. You may wish to begin this unit by finding out how much your students know about African-American music and culture in the United States.

LISTEN

African-American Music and Culture in the United States

•Assess how much of the following history your students know.

1619 - first African slaves brought to Jamestown, VA

1659 to 1705 - the term "Negro slave" appears; slavery becomes hereditary; Virginia law treats slaves as "real estate" property

1790 - census counted 700,000 slaves in southern states

➡ slaves not permitted to play drums for fear of communication and escape

PERFORM

1800 to 1860 - People like Frederick Douglass, Harriet Tubman and Sojourner Truth led the fight to abolish slavery

➡ spirituals, work songs and various forms of dance songs; 1830s minstrel show established "Jim Crow" caricatures and tried to imitate black music

1861-1865 and after - Civil War; Lincoln's Emancipation Proclamation; Negro colleges established after the war; black men gained vote

DESCRIBE

1896 - U.S. Supreme Court upheld legal segregation; by 1908 southern states had effectively deterred black men from voting

1900 to 1954 - NAACP founded; after WWI (1918) many blacks moved north to jobs in big industry; housing/school segregation continued

➡ ragtime, jazz, blues, and gospel become popular forms of music with both blacks and whites; 1920s "race" records featured black performers

CREATE

1954 to present - civil rights struggle of Martin Luther King and others outlaws school, housing, voting and other forms of segregation; many black mayors and legislative representatives elected

➡ rhythm & blues influences early rock 'n' roll; rise of soul, reggae, rap; African and Hispanic music add new vitality

---

RESOURCES

Books

Courlander, Harold. *Negro Folk Music, U.S.A.* New York: Columbia University Press, 1963.

Katz, Bernard. *The Social Implications of Early Negro Music in the United States.* New York: Arno Press and New York Times, 1969.

Southern, Eileen. *The Music of Black Americans: A History.* New York: W.W. Norton, 1971.

Southern, Eileen. *Readings in the Music of Black Americans.* New York: W.W. Norton, 1975.

Leadbelly's Life

Down in Louisiana

Huddie Ledbetter was born in 1885 in Mooringsport, Louisiana, in the bayous of the Mississippi Delta close to the Texas border. His father Wes was a hardworking sharecropper who taught him to plow and pick cotton. **"Cotton Fields"** (p. 32) and **"Bring Me L'il' Water, Silvy"** (p. 47) are musical sketches from his early life working in the fields as the son of a cotton farmer. His mother Sally was half African American and half Cherokee. Huddie's uncle Terrell, a major influence on his musical life, taught him to play first the "windjammer" Cajun accordion, then the guitar, mandolin, harmonica (mouth harp) and piano.

By age fifteen he had become a well known local musician who played at **sookey-jumps** (Saturday night country dance parties) and **breakdowns** (dances). During this period he visited Fannin Street, the entertainment district of Shreveport, and it was there that he heard many new kinds of music such as **barrel-house piano** (a form of early blues). Leadbelly was a favorite with the ladies and was known for his quick temper. Throughout his life, he worked hard, played hard, and his quick temper often got him into trouble with the law. In 1905 he left Louisiana and was "banished away and went out in West Texas, pickin' cotton."

In Texas, Leadbelly met **Blind Lemon Jefferson**, one of the great country blues guitarists and singers. Eventually Jefferson and Leadbelly worked as a musical team and played in Dallas and the surrounding countryside. Leadbelly learned many songs from Lemon Jefferson and used this collaboration to hone his guitar techniques to a fine edge. In Dallas, Leadbelly was introduced to the **12-string guitar** (a common instrument with Mexican folk musicians of the area, but not common among blues players). He also developed the technique of playing **slide guitar** (sometimes known as **bottleneck guitar**) with a knife blade.

In 1917, Leadbelly killed a man in a fight over a woman and was sentenced to a Texas prison farm. Life working on a prison chain gang was unbearably hard, and treatment of African-American prisoners was often cruel and inhuman. Since Leadbelly had lived a life of hard work and was an exceptionally strong man, he vowed to meet the prison challenge head-on and become a survivor. Because of his superior strength, he rose to the position of lead man on many of the chain gangs. The song **"Take This Hammer"** (p. 43) is a good example of a prison work song. The word "(wah)" inserted in this song indicates the point where the axe or hammer was struck while singing the song. In the evenings Leadbelly sang his songs for other prisoners. The song **"The Midnight Special"** (p. 41) was composed while Leadbelly was working in the Sugar Land prison farm.

The Texas prison worksong repertory had a big influence on blues singers such as Leadbelly and Blind Lemon Jefferson. Songs such as "Ain't No More Cane on the Brazos," "Roberta," "Long Hot Summer Days," "Shorty George" and "Make a Longtime Man Feel Bad" became an important part of Leadbelly's songbag. Some of the blues protest songs helped African Americans find a voice to express their anger over racial prejudice and discrimination.

Leadbelly's talent caught the ear of the prison warden and others working at the prison, and he was asked to play for special occasions. When he heard that the new Texas Governor Pat Neff and his wife were coming to the prison for a visit, he wrote a special song asking the governor to pardon him.

✔ Students will sing and learn about **work songs** and their function with African-American culture and in other facets of American life.

Work Songs

LISTEN

•Listen to Sweet Honey In the Rock sing "Bring Me L'il' Water, Silvy"; then have students list some reasons why people sing when they work:
- –relieving boredom or the strain of hard work
- –adding rhythm to the job being done
- –using music to help a group coordinate their work

PERFORM

•Sing **"Take This Hammer"** (p. 43) without any accompaniment except a very loud clap on the syllable "(wah)" where a hammer or axe would normally fall. This will be more realistic if the students stand, spread out and actually pretend they are swinging an axe (See photo on p. 20.). [Note: If the teacher can really get into this, students may think it's weird, but they will never forget it.] Add strong, rhythmic strumming patternson guitars or Autoharps as accompaniment to the singing. Listen to Mississippi John Hurt's "Spike Driver Blues" which uses some of these same verses.

•Other work songs to sing or listen to include:

In *Folk Songs of North America* - "Long John" (p. 537), "Another Man Done Gone" (p. 538) and "Let the Deal Go Down" (p. 548).

DESCRIBE

Listen to Stan Rogers' modern work song "The White Collar Holler" which parodies the traditional track-lining song "Oh Boys, Can't You Line 'Em."

•The American **sea shanty** tradition favored Irish- and African-Americans for the job of shantyman (song leader). Throughout the 19th century days of sailing ships, primarily **call-and-response** work songs were sung with alternation of the shantyman and the crew. The four basic types of sea shanties are:

CREATE

capstan - for hauling in the anchor (steady beat)
short haul - for small jobs like pumping out the ship (usually steady beat) **halyard** - for raising sail (crew pulls on ropes at end of response)
forecastle (pronounced "folk-sil") - leisure-time songs for crew's quarters

Sing Master #10 (TG-59) and other unaccompanied sea shanties from *Folk Songs of North America* such as "Shenandoah" (p. 53), "Blood Red Roses" (p. 54) and "A Long Time Ago" (p. 55). Refer to Colcord's *Songs of American Sailormen* for an indispensable collection of songs and descriptions of the types of work done on ships.

RESOURCES

Books

Lomax, Alan. *Folksongs of North America in the English Language.* New York: Doubleday, 1960.

Colcord, Joanna C. *Songs of American Sailormen.* New York: W.W. Norton, 1938.

Recordings

Stan Rogers: Between the Breaks . . . Live. Fogarty's Cove 002.

Sweet Honey in the Rock: Live at Carnegie Hall. Flying Fish 106.

Best of Mississippi John Hurt. Vanguard 19/20.

Nineteen hundred and twenty-three,
The judge took my liberty away from me,
Left my wife wringin' her hand and cryin',
"Lord have mercy on this man of mine."

I am your servant compose this song,
Please Governor Neff, lemme go back home,
I know my wife will jump and shout,
Train rolls up, I come stepping out.

Please, Honorable Governor, be good an' kind,
If I don't get a pardon will you cut my time?
Had you, Governor Neff, like you got me,
Wake up in the morning and I'd set you free.

The song touched the heart of the governor, who was trying to correct some of the Texas prison problems, and he pardoned Leadbelly in 1925. After release from prison, Leadbelly returned to his home in Louisiana.

Living at home in Louisiana did not bring Huddie Ledbetter peace, and within five years he was involved in a fight defending himself from an attack and was again sentenced to prison. Three years later in 1933, John Lomax, a folksong collector from the Library of Congress, visited the Angola Prison Farm where Leadbelly was located. Lomax and his son Alan were recording African-American prison work songs. The Lomaxes found Leadbelly to be an incredible source of song material from work songs to blues, dance songs, children's songs and ballads. John Lomax took a special interest in Leadbelly's case and helped get him a parole when he hand delivered another original Leadbelly song plea to Louisiana Governor Allen.

Off to New York

I was born and raised i' the country, mamma,
but I'm stayin' in town . . . in New York City,
what I'm talkin' 'bout.

The Lomaxes convinced Leadbelly to travel with them to other prisons throughout the South for the purpose of recording for the Library of Congress. Shortly thereafter Leadbelly married Martha Promise and went with the Lomaxes to Washington, D. C. and then to New York City. The song **"The Bourgeois Blues"** (p. 31) describes Leadbelly's feelings about the housing discrimination to which he and Martha were subjected on their travels.

During his stay in New York from 1935 to 1949, Leadbelly made recordings for Columbia, Capitol, Victor, Asch, Musicraft, Disc and the Library of Congress. He sang on radio programs such as *Folk Songs of America* (WNYC) and *Back Where I Come From* (CBS Radio Network). Leadbelly toured extensively throughout the Northeast and sang concerts of his music at colleges and universities. He was much in demand in New York City for appearances at local parties, lofts, clubs and political rallies. He was a favorite with the liberals and often appeared at folk gatherings with singers such as Paul Robeson, Josh White, Sonny Terry, Brownie McGhee, Woody Guthrie (they called themselves the "Headline Singers"), Burl Ives and the Almanac Singers.

Despite Leadbelly's talent and fine recordings, he was somewhat out of step with the times. During the late 1930s and '40s other blues guitarists such as Muddy Waters were moving into a style that would be called **rhythm and blues (R&B)** or **urban blues**. This emerging style was built around a small band concept which featured electric guitar with other instruments such as saxophones, piano, bass and drums. In addition to the instrumentation, the subject matter of the songs was much more concerned with urban living than the rural life described in many of Leadbelly's songs. As a result of this shift in public tastes, Leadbelly often found himself having to work at menial jobs in order to earn a living. During these years he was kept on a recording retainer by Moe Asch of Folkways Records, and in 1948 he recorded his historic *Leadbelly's Last Sessions* (FW241). At sixty-four, Huddie Ledbetter died of "Lou Gehrig's disease" in a New York hospital.

Six months after his death, his song **"Goodnight Irene"** (p. 36) became a popular hit in a version sung by the Weavers, and the record sold over two million copies. The royalties eventually started coming in, and they eased his wife Martha's financial burden. The Weavers, including Leadbelly's friend Pete Seeger, helped to popularize Leadbelly's music and eventually his songs were sung, published and recorded by many different musicians around the world.

✔ Students will learn about the African-American blues traditions through singing, listening, composing and playing.

I Got the Blues

LISTEN

• A brief history of the blues (with overlapping dates)

country blues (1900-1930s+) - solo male guitar-playing singers mostly from the Mississippi Delta and from Texas

–Robert Johnson, Blind Lemon Jefferson, Charlie Patton, Blind Blake, Mississippi John Hurt, Leadbelly, Lightnin' Hopkins

classic blues (1920-1940+) - female singer with small band; more city-oriented lyrics; mixed with jazz instrumentalists

–Bessie Smith ("Empress of the blues"), Clara Smith, Ma Rainey, Billie Holliday; tradition extends to Ella Fitzgerald, Sara Vaughan

PERFORM

urban blues (1940-1950s+) - also known as **rhythm & blues** (R&B); solo singer with small band of electric guitar, bass, drums, piano, saxophones, sometimes trumpets.

–Muddy Waters, B.B. King, Howlin' Wolf, Bo Diddley, Walter Jacobs, Sonny Boy Williamson, Elmore James, Jimmy Reed, Willie Dixon

DESCRIBE

• Have students sing and play the 12-bar blues on Master #11 (TG-60); then have them compose some of their own verses.

Point out that the open measures (3-4, 7-8 and 11-12) at the end of each phrase are where instrumentalists add **fills**—short solos in open spaces. In fact you could say that the singer and answering instrumental fill is a form of **call and response**.

➡ You can sometimes get students to improvise fills by having them use kazoos. Fills can also begin with 2, 3 or 4 "no-fault" notes as introduced in the *Rock Trax-1* guitar book and cassette.

CREATE

After you have helped students discover the **AAB** form of the lyrics, it is often helpful to brainstorm **B** lines together. Begin by having someone volunteer an A line; then have the class make up 8 to 10 B lines that would work. Help them to see that the lines usually end on the first beat of the third measure.

• Sing **"The Bourgeois Blues"** (p. 31) and ask students how it is different from the 12-bar blues model they have been studying.

• Relate 12-bar blues to its many uses in early rock 'n' roll songs of the '50s.

RESOURCES

Books

Urban Blues for Guitar. Milwaukee: Hal Leonard, 1988.

Schmid, Will. *Rock Trax-1.* Milwaukee: Hal Leonard, 1985. book and cassette

Silverman, Jerry. *Blues: An Anthology.* New York: Da Capo Press, 1985.

Recordings

The Country Blues. Folkways RF01.

Sonny Terry & Brownie McGhee Sing. Folkways 40011.

The Blues Vol. 1-4. Chess 9353, 9267, 9276, 9290 [urban blues].

The Bessie Smith Story Vol. 2-3. Columbia 856, 857.

Videos

The Blues According to Lightnin' Hopkins. Les Blank Flower Film's. (31')

Blues Like Showers of Rain. Rhapsody Films. (30')

Leadbelly's Music

Leadbelly's music reflected his growing-up years in rural Louisiana, his years of hard prison labor, and his experience with the big cities. Some of the songs that reflect his rural upbringing include "Bring Me Li'l Water, Silvy," "Boll Weevil," "Cotton Fields," and "Gray Goose" (sung by Sweet Honey in the Rock on the *A Vision Shared* recording and Leadbelly on *Folkways: The Original Vision*).

Because Leadbelly played for sookey-jumps, many of his songs have a distinct dance beat often including a strong bass line resembling a **boogie-woogie** pattern. Leadbelly introduced the ballad of "John Henry," the steel-drivin' man, in the following way:

Now this is "John Henry" and it's a dance tune
and we dance it down home and
I'm gonna play it for you.

Leadbelly pioneered a powerful bass-melody, 12-string guitar style that became the African-American counterpart to the bass-melody style of guitar pioneered by Maybelle Carter of the Carter Family and later picked up by Woody Guthrie. Other dance tunes played and sung by Leadbelly include "Corn Bread Rough" and "Salty Dog."

Most African-American singers and songwriters including Leadbelly have been influenced in some way by the church, spiritual or gospel traditions. Introducing the song "Look Away to Heaven" Leadbelly said:

At home when I go to the Baptist church,
the sisters in the amen corner,
they always lead out.

It is not uncommon for a blues or secular singer to also be involved in the world of gospel music. Two outstanding examples would be **Thomas Dorsey**—"the father of African American gospel"—who was an outstanding blues composer and pianist, and **Aretha Franklin**—"soul sister number one"—who is at home with rock or "Amazing Grace." Other Leadbelly songs that reflect this gospel tradition include "We Shall Walk Through the Valley" and "They Hung Him On a Cross."

Leadbelly's prison experiences yielded some of his most powerful songs. In addition to "The Midnight Special" and "Take This Hammer," there is "Black Betty," "Didn't Old John" (a work song influenced by the spiritual tradition), "Go Down Old Hannah," "Julie Ann Johnson" and "On a Monday."

The blues songs including "Good Morning Blues," "The Bourgeois Blues" (p. 31), "Jailhouse Blues" and "Leavin' Blues" are some of Leadbelly's best material. Leadbelly said:

. . . when you lay down at night, turn from one side of the bed all night to the other and you can't sleep, what's the matter? Blues got you. Or when you get up in the mornin', sit on side of the bed—may have a mother or father, sister or brother, boy friend or girl friend, husband or a wife around—you don't want no talk out of um. They ain't done you nothin', you ain't done them nothin'—what's the matter? Blues got you.

Leadbelly, like Woody Guthrie, loved playing and singing for children. Some of his children's songs include "Red Bird," "Ha Ha This A-Way" and a cowboy song from his horse-breaking days in Texas called "Cow Cow Yicky Yicky Yea."

In the book *The Leadbelly Songbook*, Frederic Ramsey Jr. describes Leadbelly's singing in the following way:

Leadbelly's voice was not beautiful. It was rough and grainy, and some of its raw tones came up as if scraped out of his throat. It rang out with intensity because he often shouted with violence. It had a nasal twang. The excitement he engendered came from his understanding of each melody he sang and from a strong, precise sense of rhythm. He played his own twelve-string guitar, and its tempo fell in with each type of song; for breakdowns, the strings zinged at breakneck time; but he held the slow blues to an even, carefully marked beat, usually in low register. Leadbelly was set apart from other folk singers by his extraordinary ability to tell a story, and a repertoire that included blues, work songs, slave songs, shouts, hollers, reels, railroad and prison songs, ballads, spirituals, cowboy, popular, and play songs. And above all, he was not afraid—not afraid to run up and down a scale that took in baritone and tenor registers along the way, but didn't stick to either. The hollers he yelled out were almost impossible of notation in our Occidental music scale. He was not afraid to shift pitch, and he often accelerated tempo to suit mood and action.

LISTEN

✔ Students will listen to Leadbelly's original recordings and learn more about his singing and playing style.

King of the 12-string Guitar

•Listen to songs from the *Folkways: The Original Vision* recording.

"4, 5, and 9" - with Sonny Terry and Brownie McGhee

This is a good example of a typical variation on 12-bar blues where the singer repeats the second phrase (bars 5-8) to stretch the form out to 16 bars with AAAB lyrics. Ask students to listen to the recording and discover what is different from the usual 12-bar form. Note that the players return to 12 bars on the instrumental.

PERFORM

"Fannin Street"

This recording should convince students why Leadbelly was known as the "King of the 12-string Guitar." Fannin Street was the red-light district of Shreveport, LA where Leadbelly started his public performing career.

"The Bourgeois Blues"

On this recording you can hear one of hallmarks of Leadbelly's 12-string guitar style—the use of bass runs that sound like **boogie woogie**. Play some recordings of other piano or big-band boogie woogie for comparison. Point out that boogie woogie is another form of 12-bar blues.

DESCRIBE

Another interesting facet of this recording is the irregularity of Leadbelly's phrases. Point out that this happened frequently when country blues players were not playing with anyone else. One has to be regular only in a group ensemble or band context.

"Gray Goose"

Call and response is probably the most important musical form found in African and African-American music, and "Gray Goose" is a perfect example of it. You can also hear good examples of call and response songs such as "Grizzily Bear" on the *Negro Prison Camp Work Songs* recording or "Stewball" on *Leadbelly's Last Sessions*.

CREATE

"Midnight Special"

This is one of Leadbelly's best known songs, and the use of boogie bass runs is very clear. Compare Leadbelly's recording with that of Taj Mahal on *A Vision Shared*.

RESOURCES

Recordings

Barrelhouse Boogie. RCA 8334.

Boogie Blues: Women Sing and Play Boogie Woogie. Roset 1309.

Leadbelly's Last Sessions. Folkways 2941, 2942.

Negro Prison Camp Work Songs. Folkways 4475.

Leadbelly's Influence

Leadbelly's influence started in New York. His associations with Woody Guthrie, Sonny Terry, Cisco Houston, Brownie McGhee, Paul Robeson, Burl Ives, the Almanac Singers, Oscar Brand, and others helped lay the foundations for the Folk Revival of the 1950s. On the *Folkways: The Original Vision* recording, Leadbelly collaborates with Guthrie, Houston and Terry on the song, "We Shall Be Free." Woody Guthrie was impressed by Leadbelly's ready sense of rhyme and his ability to sing for any crowd:

> I've heard him say to a padded roomful of upper class folks, "You folks are mine, I'll sing for you fine." And heard him yell out above the wild smokey clatter of an odd colored, loose nail, rattle board room packed with the freest of prancing dancers, " You folks are my best, I'll sing your request." I've seen him laugh and joke with school kids, nursery kids, little toddlers climbing all over his guitar and up and down his arms and legs, and tell them, "You make me feel new, I'll sing best for you."

Pete Seeger became a champion of Leadbelly's music and guitar styling. He published *The 12-String Guitar as Played by Leadbelly*, and with the Weavers, popularized many of Leadbelly's songs during the 1950s and '60s. Seeger comments on Leadbelly's influence on him—

> Looking back, I think that the most important thing I learned from him was the straightforward approach, the direct honesty. He bequeathed to us also, it is true, a couple hundred of the best songs any of us will ever know.

The Liverpool pop singer Lonnie Donnegan reworked many of Leadbelly's songs to create the skiffle band sound, and many of the '60s English rock groups such as the Beatles grew up playing them.

Alan Lomax, folklorist, author and friend, had this to say about him:

> Leadbelly left his mark on his era; his steel voice, his steel arm on the twelve strings and his high-voltage personality captured audiences everywhere. More than any other singer, he demonstrated to a streamlined, city-oriented world that America had living folk music— swamp primitive, angry, freighted with great sorrow and great joy.

Unit Review

REVIEW QUESTIONS

1. How do the songs "Bring Me Li'l' Water, Silvy," "Cotton Fields," "Take This Hammer" and "The Midnight Special" reflect Leadbelly's life in Louisiana and Texas?

2. Who influenced Leadbelly's musical style? What instruments did he play?

3. How does the song "The Bourgeois Blues" deal with racial discrimination? Can you find other songs about this subject?

4. Who were some of the musicians influenced by Leadbelly?

5. What are the differences you hear and see between the songs of Leadbelly and those of Woody Guthrie?

MORE ABOUT LEADBELLY

If you would like to read more about Leadbelly and hear more of his music, try these:

Asch, Moses and Alan Lomax, eds. *The Leadbelly Songbook.* New York: Oak, 1962.

Leadbelly. New York: Trio Folkways Music, 1976. —a songbook

Lomax, John A. and Alan. *Negro Folksongs as Sung by Lead Belly.* New York: MacMillan, 1936.

Leadbelly's Last Sessions. (Folkways Records 2941 A/B, C/D; 2942 A/B, C/D).

Recordings —see listing of other Leadbelly recordings on liner notes to *Folkways: The Original Vision.* Smithsonian Folkways.

CREATIVE PROJECTS

• Try making up a 12-bar blues in the style of "The Bourgeois Blues" (p. 31). Remember Leadbelly's description of the blues on page 22, and sing about whatever's got you down.

• Make up new 2-line verses for "Rock Island Line" (p. 42), keeping in mind that they can be borrowed from most African-American spirituals (See page 6 for more information.)

✔ Students will learn about the '50s and '60s folk revival through listening, singing and playing.

LISTEN

The Folk Revival

•Help students discover the age of the **coffee house** and **hootenanny** that helped lay the groundwork for the social protest of the 1960s and beyond.

The folk revival was born in the 1950s—a decade typified by the cold war, the McCarthy hearings, and books like *The Man in the Gray Flannel Suit*. Until rock 'n' roll burst on the scene in 1955, the pop music of the day was a mixture of love ballads and "easy listening" dance tunes. Whenever popular music gets too bland, someone digs back into one of the "root" traditions such as blues, folk, gospel, or ethnic music and brings a new "old" vitality to the contemporary scene.

PERFORM

The folk revival (as well as rock 'n' roll) offered songs with real content and a transfusion from African- and European-American folk music.

➡ An interesting way to pursue this topic with a current bent would be to ask students what is happening in the area of rock. Is it suffering from reruns of '50s, '60s or '70s material with no new directions? What are performers doing to refresh their music? What root traditions are they dipping into? Examples:

Paul Simon - use of S. African, Brazilian, Cajun, etc.
Peter Townshend & John Entwistle (The Who) - Non-Western
Mickey Hart (The Grateful Dead) - Non-Western percussion

DESCRIBE

•Listen to some of the songs by The Weavers.

Listen to songs from *The Weavers Greatest Hits* including Leadbelly's "Goodnight Irene."

•Dig into some of the music of Take 6, Tracy Chapman, Taj Mahal, or Sweet Honey in The Rock—African-American singers who use folk roots in their music.

CREATE

✔ **Assessment**

•Use Master #14 (TG-63) to help assess students' understanding of Unit Three (and Two). Other assessment vehicles might include performance, composition projects, listening analysis, essays or research reports.

•Master #15 (TG-64) may be used with Unit Four—*The New Generation*.

RESOURCES

Recordings

Tracy Chapman: Crossroads. Elektra 60888.

Tracy Chapman. Elektra 60774.

Mickey Hart: At the Edge. RYKO Racs 0124.

Paul Simon: Graceland. Warner Bros. WB 25447-4.

Paul Simon: The Rhythm of the Saints. Warner Bros. WB 26098-4.

Sweet Honey in The Rock: Believe I'll Run On . . .

See What the End's Gonna Be. Redwood 3500.

Sweet Honey in The Rock: Feel Something Drawing Me On. Flying Fish 375.

Take 6: So Much 2 Say. Reprise 25892-4.

Taj Mahal: Mo' Roots. Columbia 33051.

Taj Mahal: Oooh So Good'n Blues. Columbia 32600.

The Weavers Greatest Hits. Vanguard 15/16.

Singing and Playing the Songs in the Student Text

LISTEN

The most important thing you can do with the songs in the Student Text is to bring them to life and help students to make the songs their own.

Here is some good advice from Woody Guthrie—

"Please, please, please, don't read nor sing my songs like no lesson book, like no text for today. But let them be a little key to sort of unlock and let down all your old bars.

PERFORM

Watch the kids. Do like they do. Act like they act. Yell like they yell. Dance the way you see them dance. Sing like they sing. Work and rest the way the kids do.

You'll be healthier. You'll feel wealthier. You'll talk wiser. You'll go higher, do better and live longer here amongst us, if you'll just only jump in here and swim around in these songs and do like the kids do.

I don't want the kids to be grownup. I want to see the grown folks be kids."

DESCRIBE

These songs will come to life more if you sing them in context. Here are some suggestions that might help.

For example, if you were doing "I Ain't Got No Home" or "Going Down the Road" you could—

•**Have students read the related material in the Student Text** such as the section in Unit Two on the Dust Bowl (p. 14).

•**Bring in related resources** such as the book *Hard Hitting Songs for Hard-Hit People* or WPA photographs by people like Dorothea Lange.

CREATE

•**Ask students to talk to people** who lived through the experience of the Great Depression, and **use this as a springboard to lively discussion.** Don't shy away from controversial topics—they help students to understand that music is at the center of life, not on the periphery (See TG-23).

•**Watch the video tape *A Vision Shared*** in small segments related to the songs you are doing.

•**Listen to the songs on the *Folkways: The Original Vision* recording,** and compare them to the versions on the video tape and in the Student Text. Students will be interested in talking about the use of electric guitars and other amplified instruments used by the *A Vision Shared* performers.

•**Sing, play, and listen to related songs suggested in the Teacher's Guide.**

•**Give students ownership in the songs** by having them **create** new verses or compose new songs on a related topic.

•**Sing the songs with gusto using instruments such as guitars or Autoharps to create good folk/rock accompaniments.**

Instrumental Accompaniments to the Songs

LISTEN

On page 48 of the Student Text is a **Guitar Chord Chart** that illustrates all of the chords used in the songs on pages 31-47.

Songs are pitched in **keys that are both easy to sing and easy to play** on folk instruments. You should feel free to move songs to a different key if necessary.

A **guitar capo** is a valuable tool that helps students find a key in which they can both play and sing. For that reason, you will find the words *Option: Capo 2 or 3* in the upper left corner of some songs. Remember . . . this is just a suggestion. Also, feel free to use the capo on songs where it is not listed as an option.

PERFORM

•An interesting possibility presents itself on a song like "The Bourgeois Blues." If the guitarists play in the key of A and place their capos at the 3rd fret, the guitars sound in the key of C (Each fret on the guitar is a half-step.). This offers several other advantages—

– It is a good singing key.

–Pianos and Autoharps can play in the easy key of C.

–Guitarists can avoid the "dreaded" F(7) chord that only becomes easy when they reach an intermediate level.

DESCRIBE

–Guitarists can play a blues bass shuffle or fill-in blues licks in the Key of A.

You might wish to create a class **jug band**, **skiffle band**, or **string band** composed of the following types of instruments (if available):

•guitars, Autoharps, banjos, fiddles, dulcimers, string bass or electric bass, washboard (played with metal thimbles or spoons), gutbucket (washtub bass), spoons (played back-to-back with an index finger between the handles), jug, and kazoos.

CREATE

•You can make a **gutbucket** or **washtub bass** by going to the hardware store and buying a medium-sized washtub and some clothes-line rope. While you're there, get a washboard. Turn the washtub upside down; then punch a small hole in the center with a nail. Pass the clothes-line rope through the hole, and tie a knot at the end to keep the rope securely attached to the bottom of the washtub. Then find an old broom handle or closet hanger pole which is approximately 4-to-5 feet long. Notch one end so that it rests securely on the edge of the washtub. Put a nail or screw in the other end of the pole and tie the clothes line rope to it as in the illustration below. When a student plays the washtub bass, he or she should wear a glove on the plucking hand and rest one foot on the outer rim of the washtub to keep it in place.

The Bourgeois Blues
page 31

The "Bourgeois Blues" is a 12-bar blues that speaks directly about the practice of segregated facilities for blacks and whites in America before the 1950s/'60s civil-rights legislation.

•You may find it useful to review with students the changing labels—"Negro, colored, black, Afro-Americans, and African Americans"—that have been used to describe members of Leadbelly's race.

Point of Interest—The NAACP [National Association for the Advancement of Colored People] has not changed its name since its beginnings in the early 1900s.

•If guitars capo at the 3rd fret, pianos and Autoharps can play in C.

•Notice that the lyrics do not conform to the usual 12-bar blues formula found on Master #10. Also, there is no IV chord in bar 10.

•Guitars in A may wish to play a blues bass shuffle pattern or a boogie woogie bass pattern.

Cotton Fields
page 32

"Cotton Fields" is a song about the kind of work Leadbelly grew up doing in the fields of Louisiana and Texas.

•Sing and play this song like a dance tune: at a fairly fast pace with lots of rhythmic vitality and syncopation.

•This would be a good piece to do with a jug or skiffle band. Have the band take an instrumental break, featuring various instruments such as the washboard or spoons, between some of the verses.

•Help students discover the hidden call-and-response form (the response is "in them old cotton fields back home") built into this song.

Deportee
page 33

As explained by Arlo Guthrie on the *A Vision Shared* video tape, "Deportee" was written for a group of Mexican migrant workers whose plane went down as they were being deported back to Mexico. While Woody Guthrie was in California, he spent time learning songs from migrant workers and singing about them.

•The style of this song has much of the charm of many Mexican songs in 3/4 time. To add more of that flavor, add a harmony part to the chorus by singing a third below the melody except for the last phrase, where the harmony should move above the melody. Listen to recordings such as Linda Ronstadt's *Canciones de mi padre* (Elektra 60765) to hear the typical parallel-third type of harmony found throughout Hispanic cultures.

•If possible, add mandolins or guitars playing the melody (and harmony) an octave higher as an instrumental break. This piece can also be played by dulcimers in DAA tuning.

Do Re Mi
page 34

"Do Re Mi" is often chosen as one of the best representatives of Woody's Dust Bowl ballads (for example, it is included in the *Smithsonian Collection of Classic Country Music*).

•This is another good jug- or string-band piece as is well illustrated on the video tape.

•Students will want to know more about several of the instruments used on the *A Vision Shared* video tape.

—The vest-shaped washboard comes from the Zydeco tradition. This style, featuring accordion and other instruments, can be heard on recordings by Clifton Chenier or Queen Ida.

—The guitar played flat on the lap is a **Dobro**—a forerunner of the **pedal steel** often heard on contemporary country recordings.

—The mouth keyboard is called a Melodica, and the pear-shaped guitar is actually a tenor mandolin which has 4 double sets of strings.

Going Down the Road
page 35

"Going Down the Road" is another Depression classic.

•Lee Hays, who collaborated with Woody on this song, was a member of the Weavers.

•This is a perfect song for making up new verses. Students only need to make up one line, and it doesn't have to rhyme with anything.

•For more verses see *Hard Hitting Songs for Hard-Hit People* (p. 216).

•Are there segments of our society who are still "looking for a job with honest pay"?

Goodnight Irene
page 36

"Goodnight Irene" became a popular song shortly after Leadbelly died.

•Listen to Leadbelly's version on the *Folkways: The Original Vision* recording; then compare it to—

– the music in the Student Text

—Brian Wilson's version on the *A Vision Shared* recording

—The Weavers' version on *The Weavers Greatest Hits* (Vanguard 15/16)

•Sing both "Ramblin' 'Round" and "Roll On, Columbia" (p. 47) —Woody Guthrie's new sets of words based on Leadbelly's "Goodnight Irene."

•Have students make up new verses.

•On the chorus, sing harmony that is a parallel third above the melody. This is one of the best harmony-by-ear songs of all time.

Hard Travelin'
page 37

"Hard Travelin' " is an account of Woody's trip across working America.

•Sing the song in two beats per measure at a fairly fast pace .

•The second verse is about riding "the rods" (the steam trains).

•This song is pitched just right for use in either a **banjo solo** (5-string bluegrass banjos are tuned from the bass string D G B D G) or as a **Carter style bass-melody solo on guitar**, which is what Woody played. (This style is based on the playing of Maybelle Carter of the Carter Family—one of the pioneering families of Hillbilly music in the 1920s.)

Hobo's Lullaby
page 38

"Hobo's Lullaby" by Goebel Reeves was Woody's favorite song.

•Compare the version on the *A Vision Shared* video tape with Woody's on the *Folkways: The Original Vision* recording.

•This song has much of the nostalgia found in the sentimental ballads of the 19th century Civil War period. An interesting comparison would be "Just Before the Battle, Mother," which begins with a similar melody.

•Here is another really sentimental verse that is sometimes sung to this tune—

> Do not let your heart be troubled
> If the world calls you a bum,
> 'Cause if your mother'd lived, she'd love you,
> You are still your mother's son.

•On the chorus, teach students how to sing a harmony part that is mostly a parallel third above the melody.

I Ain't Got No Home
page 39

"I Ain't Got No Home" is a timeless song about the tragedy of the dispossessed.

•See page TG-25 for a detailed plan for dealing with the homeless theme.

•Compare Bruce Springsteen's melody and arrangement of this song with the original. This a good illustration of how a folk song can be considerably modified to suit another performing style, such as rock.

•Discuss how the line "the gamblin' man is rich and the workin' man is poor" could be applied to people who "gamble" on a large scale, such as those involved in stock or savings and loan scandals.

I've Got to Know
page 40

"I've Got to Know" comes out of a period around World War II when Woody was raising some big questions about how the world works.

•On the *A Vision Shared* video tape, Sweet Honey in The Rock begins with the old gospel standard "Further Along," which has a melody that is similar to "I've Got to Know."

•Perform the song with three beats per measure. You may wish to reinforce the 9/8 meter signature by playing a recording of Bach's *Jesu, Joy of Man's Desiring*, which is also in 9/8 time.

•This is a good example of a melody based on the major pentatonic mode (Do Re Mi Sol La).

•You can teach your students how to sing a lower harmony part for the chorus. Show them that when the melody uses the 5th of the triad (D - F# - A), the harmony usually falls below the melody. Start in unison on the first two notes; for the harmony, stay on F# when the melody moves up to A, and move in parallel thirds after that until the phrase ends in unison. Repeat that process for the other phrases.

The Midnight Special
page 41

"The Midnight Special" is one of Leadbelly's songs about the prison experience.

•Strum an even eighth-note accompaniment, and make this song sound as much like rock as you can.

•A good introduction would be three measures prior to measure 1—
G / / C | G / / C | G / / C | G "Yonder comes Miss" |

•Teach your students to let some chords ring for four beats rather than continue strumming with the right hand. Two good spots for this would be the first measure (hold the G chord while you sing "Yonder comes Miss"; then continue strumming on the C chord in the next measure) and the pickups to the chorus.

Rock Island Line
page 42

"Rock Island Line" is a train song by Leadbelly.

•The most fun way to perform this song is to gradually speed up like a train. Eventually the words should fly past like telephone poles fly by your window on a speeding train. The Rock Island Line originally ran north and south from Minnesota to Texas.

•On the verse, strum only on beat one and let the chords ring through each of the first two measures; then resume strumming eighth notes vigorously on the D7 chord.

•Make up new 2-line verses in the African-American tradition (see p. TG-11) or borrow some good ones from songs like "Wade in the Water" (Master #4).

•If students don't know how to play the C7 chord, substitute the C chord.

Take This Hammer
page 43

"Take This Hammer" is an axe or hammer work song from Leadbelly's prison experience.

•Get the full feeling of this song by having students sing it unaccompanied with a loud clap on the word "(wah)."

•Stand up, spread out, and make the axe or hammer motion as you sing. Notice how the song helps you time your blow and makes the work easier.

•Another good work song with a similar feel is "Didn't Old John" from *The Leadbelly Songbook* (p. 25). "Didn't Old John" has a melody very similar to the commonly sung communion hymn "Let Us Break Bread Together," which also comes out of the African-American tradition.

•If guitars or Autoharps are used on this piece, strum a strong, even eighth-note accompaniment. If guitarists are more experienced, transpose the song up to the key of E.

This Land Is Your Land
page 44

In a recent survey of American music teachers, Woody Guthrie's "This Land Is Your Land" was the song most requested to be in elementary songbooks. Chances are that students know it already. Your main challenge (particularly in middle and high schools) will be to bring new light to bear on the song so that it doesn't seem like a "kiddie" song.

•Focus on the verses that students have never seen. Most likely the unfamiliar verses will be 5, 6 and 7.

•You can use this song as a vehicle for focusing on melodic variation by playing the end of the *A Vision Shared* video tape and listening to each of the different performers do a verse in a different way. Discuss the variations that students hear.

Union Maid
page 45

"Union Maid" is a rollicking union song to the fiddle tune "Redwing," which Woody wrote while on the road singing at union meetings around the country.

•Older students will be interested in the union movement in this country. Pete Seeger and Bob Reiser's excellent book *Carry It On* provides a good look at how songs have been right at the center of this struggle from the very beginning.

•Have them study the IWW (Industrial Workers of the World) also known as the "Wobblies," and their legendary leader and songwriter Joe Hill (who wrote "Pie in the Sky"). The *IWW Songbook* (also known as the *Little Red Songbook*) is still available for $2.50 from Elderly Instruments, P.O Box 14210, Lansing, MI 48901.

•*Hard Hitting Songs for Hard-Hit People* is full of union songs sung by legendary people like Aunt Molly Jackson.

Vigilante Man
page 46

"Vigilante Man" is Woody's song about the injustices visited upon migrant laborers during his days in California.

•In this context the word "vigilante" refers to members of the general public who took the law into their own hands and attempted to "aid" justice by harassing migrants. The word comes up again during the '40s and '50s segregation battles, when conservatives took the law into their own hands to try to preserve racial segregation.

•Bruce Springsteen breathes new life into "Vigilante Man" on the *A Vision Shared* video tape. He changes the melody and adds a hard-driving rock style. Chances are good that students will want to sing it his way. If so, learn it together from the video tape.

Bring Me Li'l' Water, Silvy
page 47

"Bring Me Li'l' Water, Silvy" is beautifully brought to life by Sweet Honey in The Rock on the *A Vision Shared* video tape.

•Sing along with the video tape; then try the song with guitar and Autoharp accompaniment.

Ramblin' 'Round
page 47

"Ramblin' 'Round" is a set of new words that Woody Guthrie wrote to the tune, "Goodnight Irene"   (p. 36).

•Notice that the last phrase repeats.

•Have students change the words of the chorus to "I always meet a friend I know" if they wish and then make up their own verses.

•This song lends itself to harmony a third above.

Roll On, Columbia
page 47

"Roll On, Columbia" is another set of words to "Goodnight Irene" (p. 36). Woody wrote it in the '40s for the Bonneville Power Administration (BPA) which was building the Grand Coulee and Bonneville dams.

•Listen to Arlo Guthrie's version of "Grand Coulee Dam" from the *A Vision Shared* video tape. This is another of the songs Woody wrote for the BPA.

THE GOLDEN VANITY

option: Capo 2 or 3

traditional English ballad

1. There was a ship that sailed____ all____ on the Low-land Sea, And the name of our ship was the Gold-en Van-i-ty, And we feared she would be tak-en by the Span-ish en-e-my As she sailed in the Low-land, Low-land, low, As she sailed____ in the Low-land Sea.

2. Then up____ stepped our cab-in boy and bold-ly out spoke he, And he said to our Cap-tain, "What would you give to me If____ I would swim a-long-side of the Span-ish en-e-my And sink her in the Low-land, Low-land, low, And____ sink her in the Low-land Sea."

3. "Oh, I would give you silver, and I would give you gold,
   And my own fairest daughter your bonny bride shall be
   If you would swim alongside of the Spanish enemy
   And sink her in the Lowland, Lowland low,
   And sink her in the Lowland Sea."

4. Then quickly he made ready and overboard sprang he,
   And he swam alongside of the Spanish enemy,
   With his brace and his auger in her side he bored holes three,
   And he sank her in the Lowland, Lowland, low,
   And he sank her in the Lowland Sea.

5. Then quickly he swam back to the cheering of the crew,
   But the Captain would not heed him for his promise he did rue,
   And he scorned his poor entreatings as loudly he did sue,
   And he left him in the Lowland, Lowland, low,
   And he left him in the Lowland Sea.

6. Then quickly he swam 'round unto the port side,
   And up unto his messmates full bitterly he cried,
   Oh messmates, draw me up, for I'm drifting with the tide,
   And I'm sinking in the Lowland, Lowland, low,
   And I'm sinking in the Lowland Sea."

7. Then his messmates drew him up, but on the deck he died,
   And they stitched him in his hammock which was so fair and wide,
   And they lowered him o'erboard, and he drifted with the tide,
   And he sank in the Lowland, Lowland, low,
   And he sank__ in the Lowland Sea.

American
Civil War
1861-1865

THE BATTLE HYMN OF THE REPUBLIC
Words by Julia Ward Howe

    G
Mine eyes have seen the glory of the coming of the Lord;
    C   G
He is trampling out the vintage where the grapes of wrath are stored;
                                        Em
He hath loosed the fateful lightning of His terrible swift sword,
    Am   D7   G
His truth is marching on.

    G   C   G
  Glory, Glory Hallelujah, Glory, Glory Hallelujah,

                        Em   Am   D7   G
  Glory, Glory Hallelujah, His truth is marching on.

Pre-Civil War
Abolition
of Slavery

JOHN BROWN'S BODY to the tune of 'The Battle Hymn'

John Brown's body lies a-mouldering in the grave,
John Brown's body lies a-mouldering in the grave,
John Brown's body lies a-mouldering in the grave,
But his soul goes marching on.

  Glory, Glory Hallelujah, Glory, Glory Hallelujah,
  Glory, Glory Hallelujah, His soul goes marching on.

John Brown died that the slaves might be free, (3 times)
His soul goes marching on.   CHORUS

Union
Movement
20th Century

SOLIDARITY FOREVER to the tune of 'The Battle Hymn'

When the union's inspiration through the workers' blood shall run,
There can be no power greater anywhere beneath the sun;
Yet what force on earth is weaker than the feeble strength of one,
For the union makes us strong.

  Solidarity Forever, Solidarity Forever,
  Solidarity Forever, For the union makes us strong.

One of the
many parodies
made up by
people like you.

GLORY, GLORY, BALMY BREEZES to the tune of 'The Battle Hymn'

I wear my silk pajamas in the summer when it's hot.
I wear my flannel nightie in the winter when it's not,
And sometimes in the springtime and sometimes in the fall
I jump between the sheets with nothing on at all.

  Glory, Glory, Hallelujah,
  Balmy breezes blowin' through ya.
  Glory, Glory, Hallelujah,
  When I jump between the sheets with nothing on at all.

AMAZING GRACE

John Newton
Sacred Harp spiritual

2. Twas grace that taught my heart to fear, And grace my fears relieved;
How precious did that grace appear, The hour I first believed!

3. Through many dangers, toils and snares, I have already come;
'Tis grace has brought me save thus far, And grace will lead me home.

The shaped note Sacred Harp spiritual version of "Amazing Grace" was printed like this.

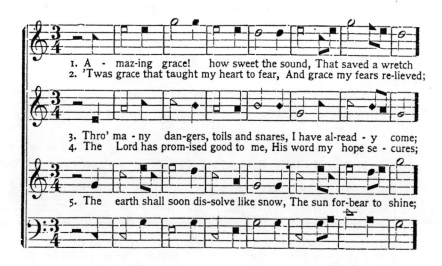

PHOTODUPLICATION OF THIS PAGE IS ALLOWED.

WADE IN THE WATER

African-American Spiritual

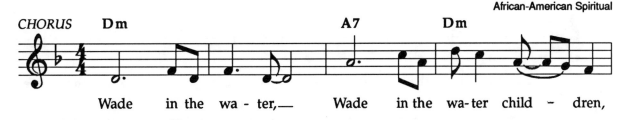

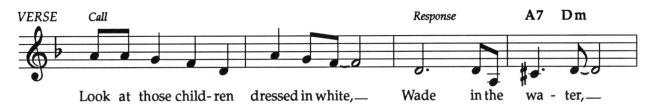

2. Down in the valley, down on my knees,   Wade in the water,
   Asking my Lord to save me please,   Wade in the water.   CHORUS

3. You can hinder me here, you can hinder me there,   Wade in the water,
   But the Lord in Heaven will hear my prayer,   Wade in the water.   CHORUS

4. One of these nights 'bout twelve o'clock,   Wade in the water,
   This old world's gonna reel and rock,   Wade in the water.   CHORUS

IT MAY BE THE LAST TIME   to the tune of "Wade in the Water"

Oh__ it may be, Oh__ it may be,___
Oh__ it may be, It may be the last time, I don't know.

Sinner better mind how you step on the cross,   It may be the last time, I don't know,
Your foot might slip and your soul get lost,   It may be the last time, I don't know.

The Bible warns you day by day,   It may be the last time, I don't know,
That you got to change your wicked way,   It may be the last time, I don't know.

This traditional African-American spiritual would lend itself well to some new verses about the environment or world peace.

ROSIN THE BEAU

popular song of 1838
based on an Irish tune

The Gold Rush of 1849 brought many settlers to the West in search of quick fortune. Once bitten by the "gold bug," they went from strike to strike in search of treasure. This ballad from the state of Washington tells how one of these miners ended up.

ACRES OF CLAMS   to the tune of "Rosin the Beau"

I've travelled all over this country, Prospecting and digging for gold,
I've tunneled, hydraulicked and cradled, And I have been frequently sold.
And I have been frequently sold. And I have been frequently sold.
I've tunneled, hydraulicked and cradled, And I have been frequently sold.

For each man who got rich by mining, Perceiving that hundreds grew poor,
I made up my mind to try farming, The only pursuit that was sure.   (Repeat as in verse 1.)

So, rolling my grub in my blanket, I left all my tools on the ground,
I started one morning to shank it, For the country they call Puget Sound.

Arriving flat broke in midwinter, I found it enveloped in fog,
And covered all over with timber, Thick as the hair on the back of a dog.

I staked me a claim in the forest, And sat myself down to hard toil,
For two years I chopped and I worked there, But I never got down to the soil.

I tried to get out of the country, But poverty forced my to stay,
Until I became an old settler, Then nothing could drive me away.

No longer the slave of ambition, I laugh at the world and its shams,
As I think of my pleasant condition, Surrounded by acres of clams.

LITTLE VANNY to the tune of "Rosin the Beau"

1840 Presidential campaign: Martin Van Buren vs. William H. Harrison— "Tippecanoe"

You can't make a song to Van Buren, Because his long name will not do;
There's nothin' about him allurin', As there is about Tippecanoe!

He never was seen in a battle, Where bullet and cannon shot flew;
His nerves would be shocked with the rattle, Of a contest like Tippecanoe!

While Harrison marched to the border, Sly Van stayed at home as you know,
Afraid of the smell of gun-powder — Then hurrah for Old Tippecanoe!

Little Mat was too tender a dandy, To shoulder a musket and go
Where Harrison battled so handy, As he did when at Tippecanoe!

But snug in his pretty silk stockings, And dressed in his broadcloth all new,
He roasted his shins in a parlor — Not fighting like Tippecanoe!

And now with his gold spoons and dishes, He lives like a king with his crew;
He'll feast on the loaves and the fishes, Till we put in Old Tippecanoe.

LINCOLN AND LIBERTY to the tune of "Rosin the Beau"

1860 Presidential campaign that elected Abraham Lincoln

Hurrah for the choice of the nation, Our chieftain so brave and so true!
We'll go for the great reformation, For Lincoln and Liberty, too.
We'll go for the son of Kentucky, The hero of Hoosierdom through,
The pride of the Suckers, so lucky, For Lincoln and Liberty, too.

They'll find what by felling and mauling, Our rail-maker statesman can do;
For the people are everywhere calling, For Lincoln and Liberty, too.
Then up with the banner so glorious, The star-spangled red, white and blue,
We'll fight 'til our banner's victorious, For Lincoln and Liberty, too.

Our David's good sling is unerring, The Slavocrat's giant he slew,
Then shout for the freedom preferring, For Lincoln and Liberty, too.
We'll go for the son of Kentucky, The hero of Hoosierdom through,
The pride of the Suckers, so lucky, For Lincoln and Liberty, too.

OLD ABE LINCOLN to the tune of "The Old Grey Mare"

1864 Presidential campaign that re-elected Abraham Lincoln

D
Old Abe Lincoln came out of the wilderness,
A7   D
Out of the wilderness, Out of the wilderness,
D   A7   D
Old Abe Lincoln came out of the wilderness, Many long years ago.
  D   G   D   G   D
  Many long years ago. Many long years ago.
D   A7   D
  Old Abe Lincoln came out of the wilderness, Many long years ago.

Old Jeff Davis tore down the government, (Repeat as in verse 1.)

But old Abe Lincoln built up a better one, (Repeat as in verse 1.)

PHOTODUPLICATION OF THIS PAGE IS ALLOWED.

THE STYLE CHART

African-American	European-American
few words – – – – – – – –	many words

① much repetition ② fewer words ③ middle ④ fairly wordy ⑤ wordy

relaxed consonants – – – – – – –	articulated consonants

① relaxed ② fairly relaxed ③ middle ④ fairly articulated ⑤ articulated

group singing – – – – – – –	solo singing

① group ② mostly group ③ mixed ④ mostly solo ⑤ solo

buzzy or raspy tone – – – – – – –	clear tone

① raspy ② fairly raspy ③ middle ④ fewer clear ⑤ clear

open-throated tone – – – – – – –	somewhat nasal tone

① open ② fairly open ③ middle ④ somewhat nasal ⑤ very nasal

syncopated rhythms – – – – – – –	on-beat rhythms

① syncopated ② fairly syncopated ③ middle ④ fairly straight ⑤ straight

3-against-2 meters – – – – – – –	one meter

① uses 3-against-2 meters ③ some 3-against-2 ⑤ one meter

obvious beat – – – – – – –	subtle or hidden beat

① strong beat ② fairly strong beat ③ middle ④ some beat ⑤ little beat

bending melody notes – – – – – – –	straight melodies

① much bending ② fairly much ③ middle ④ fairly straight ⑤ straight

much melody sliding – – – – – – –	some melody sliding

① much sliding ② fairly much ③ middle ④ fairly straight ⑤ straight

added words/syllables – – – – – – –	regular words

① many added words ③ a few added words ⑤ no added words

THE STYLE CHART

African-American	①	②	③	④	⑤	European-American
few words	①	②	③	④	⑤	many words
relaxed consonants	①	②	③	④	⑤	articulated consonants
group singing	①	②	③	④	⑤	solo singing
buzzy or raspy tone	①	②	③	④	⑤	clear tone
open-throated tone	①	②	③	④	⑤	somewhat nasal tone
syncopated rhythms	①	②	③	④	⑤	on-beat rhythms
3-against-2 meters	①		③		⑤	one meter
obvious beat	①	②	③	④	⑤	subtle or hidden beat
bending melody notes	①	②	③	④	⑤	straight melodies
much melody sliding	①	②	③	④	⑤	some melody sliding
added words/syllables	①		③		⑤	regular words

THE STYLE CHART

African-American	①	②	③	④	⑤	European-American
few words	①	②	③	④	⑤	many words
relaxed consonants	①	②	③	④	⑤	articulated consonants
group singing	①	②	③	④	⑤	solo singing
buzzy or raspy tone	①	②	③	④	⑤	clear tone
open-throated tone	①	②	③	④	⑤	somewhat nasal tone
syncopated rhythms	①	②	③	④	⑤	on-beat rhythms
3-against-2 meters	①		③		⑤	one meter
obvious beat	①	②	③	④	⑤	subtle or hidden beat
bending melody notes	①	②	③	④	⑤	straight melodies
much melody sliding	①	②	③	④	⑤	some melody sliding
added words/syllables	①		③		⑤	regular words

Key

European-American
—war protest song,
"Cruel War"

African-American
—spiritual, "Daniel"

African-American
—railroad work song,
"Can't Ya Line 'Em"

European-American
—19th century song,
"The Farmer in the
One"

African-American
—spiritual, "Oh Mary,
Don't You Weep"

European-American
—love ballad, "The
Water is Wide"

European-American
— ballad, "Darling
Corey"

European-American
—lumberjack ballad,
"Blue Mountain Lake"

African-American
—prison work song,
"Another Man Done
Gone"

African-American
—blues, "Railroad
Blues"

European-American
—Shaker song,
"Simple Gifts"

African-American
—spiritual, "Peace
Like a River"

LYRICS FROM AMERICAN SONGS

The cruel war is raging and Johnny has to fight,
I want to be with him from morning 'til night.
I want to be with him, it grieves my heart so;
Oh let me go with you: No, my love, no.

Didn't my Lord deliver Daniel?
Didn't my Lord deliver Daniel?
Didn't my Lord deliver Daniel?
Didn't my Lord deliver Daniel; then why not every man?

Oh boys, can't you line 'em, Oh boys, can't you line 'em,
Oh boys, can't you line 'em, See Eloisa come a-linin' track.
     One of these nights 'bout 12 o'clock,
     This ol' world is gonna reel and rock.

When the farmer comes to town with a wagon broken down,
Oh the farmer is the one who feeds them all,
If you'll only look and see, I think you will agree
That the farmer is the one who feeds them all.

Oh Mary don't you weep, don't you mourn,
Oh Mary don't you weep, don't you mourn,
Pharoah's army got drownded, Oh Mary don't you weep.

The water is wide, I cannot cross over,
And neither have I wings to fly,
Build me a boat that can carry two
And both shall row, my true love and I.

The next time I saw darlin' Corey
She was standin' by the banks of the sea.
She had a pistol strapped around her body
And a banjo on her knee.

Come all you good fellers, wherever you be,
Come set down a-while and listen to me;
The truth I will tell you without a mistake
About the rackets we had around Blue Mountain Lake.

Another man done gone,
Another man done gone
From the country farm,
Another man done gone.

Went down to the station and looked on the board,
Went down to the station and looked on the board,
Said bad times are comin', but better down the road.

'Tis the gift to be simple, 'tis the gift to be free,
'Tis the gift to come down where we ought to be,
And when we find ourselves in the place just right
'Twill be in the valley of love and delight.

I've got peace like a river, I've got peace like a river,
I've got peace like a river in my soul,
I've got peace like a river, I've got peace like a river,
I've got peace like a river in my soul.

HAUL AWAY, JOE

unaccompanied

traditional sea shanty

King Louie was the King of France before the Revolution,
    'Way haul a-way, we'll haul a-way, Joe.
King Louie got his head cut off which spoiled his constitution,
    'Way haul a-way, we'll haul a-way, Joe.
    CHORUS

LONESOME RIDER BLUES

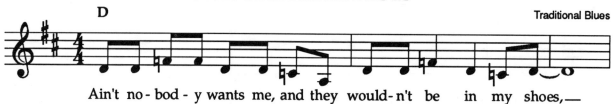

Traditional Blues

Ain't no-bod-y wants me, and they would-n't be in my shoes,—

Ain't no-bod-y wants me, and they would-n't be in my shoes,—

I feel so bad, I got the lone-some rid-er blues.—

2. If I had a-listened to what my mama said, (2x)
   I'd be home sleepin' in my nice warm feather bed.

3. River is deep and the river sure is wide, (2x)
   The woman (man) I love is on the other side.

4. Hey, baby, baby, I treated you so wrong, (2x)
   Sweet lovin' baby, I'll be missin' you 'fore long.

5. If I mistreat you, I sure don't mean no harm, (2x)
   'Cause I'm a motherless child, and I don't know right from wrong.

6. You used to be my sugar, but you ain't sweet no more. (2x)
   You got another baby hangin' 'round your door.

7. I got the blues at midnight, and they don't leave till day, (2x)
   Got to find another baby to drive those blues away.

8. I woke up this mornin', the blues all in my head. (2x)
   I rolled back the covers, the blues all in my bed.

9. Sun gonna shine on my back door someday, (2x)
   Wind gonna rise up and blow my blues away.

UNIT ONE CROSSWORD PUZZLE

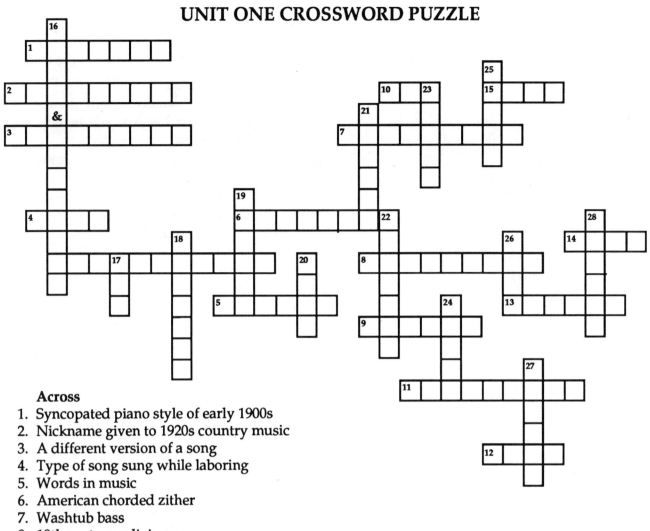

Across
1. Syncopated piano style of early 1900s
2. Nickname given to 1920s country music
3. A different version of a song
4. Type of song sung while laboring
5. Words in music
6. American chorded zither
7. Washtub bass
8. 19th century religious song
9. Wordy story song
10. Abbrev. for urban blues
11. New words to old tune printed on paper
12. Music passed by oral/aural tradition
13. Instrument with strings across a board or box
14. '60s or later popular African-American music
15. Tradition passed by "word of mouth"

Down
16. Alternation between leader and group
17. Abbrev. for 1940-50s music on Grand Ole Opry
18. Vertical element in music
19. New words to an old tune
20. Name for records by African Am. before 1949
21. String instrument with 6 or 12 strings
22. Current songs found on sheet music and CDs.
23. African-Am. song often found in 12-bar form
24. African-Am. string instr. with drum resonator
25. White recording of an African-American hit
26. African-Am. hot music played by bands
27. Another name for the violin
28. African-Am religious song—1920s on

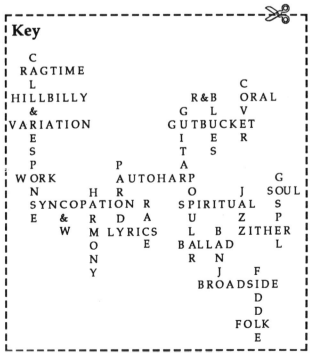

Key

```
C
RAGTIME                                      C
L                              R&B    ORAL
HILLBILLY                      G L     V
&                         GUTBUCKET
VARIATION                      I   E     R
E                              T   S
S                   P          A
P          P      AUTOHARP              G
WORK       H    R       O     J   SOUL
N          R    R   R  SPIRITUAL   S
SYNCOPATION R   D A     U   Z     S
E     &    R   D A     L   B   ZITHER
W   M LYRICS       L   B   ZITHER  L
O         E    BALLAD          L
N              R N
Y                J   F
          BROADSIDE
                 D
                 D
               FOLK
                 E
```

UNIT ONE QUIZ

Match the terms with the information in the column at the right by placing the number in the blank.

Key		
21	___	oral tradition
7	___	folk music
28	___	parody or "take-off"
18	___	ballad
13	___	broadside
2	___	call and response
35	___	African-Am. 2-line rhyme
14	___	variation
27	___	popular song
6	___	xylophone
23	___	banjo
11	___	gutbucket
20	___	African-Am. spiritual
30	___	Fisk Jubilee Singers
8	___	gospel
10	___	country blues
25	___	classic blues
33	___	urban blues
15	___	ragtime
31	___	jazz
3	___	race records
17	___	cover
22	___	soul
29	___	guitar
9	___	Autoharp
24	___	Sacred Harp spiritual
34	___	piano
26	___	fiddle tune
1	___	bluegrass
4	___	hillbilly
32	___	country and western
16	___	Grand Ole Opry
12	___	harmony
19	___	country
5	___	rock 'n' roll

1. Type of country music founded by Bill Monroe featuring acoustic guitar, banjo, fiddle, mandolin
2. Alternation between leader and group
3. Pre-1949 name for records by African Americans
4. 1920s nickname for country music
5. 1955 popular music combining C&W and R&B
6. Mallet percussion instrument found in Africa
7. Music changed by oral/aural tradition
8. New name given to religious songs in 1920s
9. American chorded zither
10. Early 20th century African-Am. complaint song—solo male singer with guitar
11. Washtub bass
12. The vertical element in music—several pitches sounded at one time
13. Parody or "take-off" printed on paper—after 1450
14. New version of a song or piece of music
15. Syncopated piano music from turn of the century
16. Nashville country radio program
17. White performer's recording of an African-Am. hit
18. Wordy story song
19. Label given to "hillbilly" and "C&W" after 1970s
20. 19th century religious song with call & response
21. Passed by "word of mouth"
22. Label given pop music by African Am.—1960s on
23. African-Am. string instrument with drum resonator
24. 19th century shaped-note hymn
25. Bessie Smith, etc. featured with small jazz band
26. Folk or bluegrass violin solo
27. Current song on sheet music and recording
28. New words to an old tune
29. Popular stringed instrument with 6 or 12 strings
30. African-Am. choral group which performed widely in the years after the Civil War
31. A type of African-Am. music which started in New Orleans—featured bands, singers, improvisation
32. 1940-50s name which replaced the term "hillbilly"
33. Rhythm and blues—1940-50s name for city music by Muddy Waters and others
34. A large European-Am. zither with 88 keys
35. "I may be right, I may be wrong, You know you'll miss me when I'm gone."

WOODY GUTHRIE AND LEADBELLY QUIZ

Key

"This Land Is Your Land"

"Ramblin' 'Round"
"Roll On, Columbia"

Pete Seeger

"Do Re Mi"
"Going Down the Road"
"Hard Travelin' "
"I Ain't Got No Home"
"Vigilante Man"

guitar, mandolin,
harmonica, fiddle

Carter Family
Jimmie Rodgers

Cisco Houston,
Sonny Terry,
Pete Seeger,
Leadbelly, Josh White

Bob Dylan

12-string Guitar

"Bring Me Li'l' Water, Silvy"
"Cotton Fields"

AAB

boogie woogie

Blind Lemon Jefferson

"The Midnight Special"
"Take This Hammer"

"Goodnight Irene"

"The Bourgeois Blues"

Fill in the blanks with the correct answer.

1. Woody Guthrie's song _____ was an answer to Irving Berlin's World War II favorite "God Bless America."

2. The melody from Leadbelly's "Goodnight Irene" was used for which two Woody Guthrie's songs? _____ and _____ .

3. _____ was a close friend of Woody Guthrie and Leadbelly. He wrote the song "Where Have All the Flowers Gone?" and was the father of the 1950s-'60s folk revival.

4. Three of Woody Guthries songs that describe some part of life during the Great Depression and Dust Bowl of the 1930s were: _____ , _____ , and _____ .

5. Three of the musical instruments that Woody Guthrie played were: _____ , _____ , and _____ .

6. Pioneers of hillbilly music who influenced Woody Guthrie's musical style were: _____ and _____ .

7. Other folk performers who played and sang with Woody Guthrie were _____ , _____ , and _____ .

8. _____ , who wrote "Song to Woody" and many great hits such as "Blowin' In the Wind," is one of many younger performers who were influenced by Woody Guthrie's musical style and life values.

9. Huddie Ledbetter, better know as Leadbelly, was also known as The King of the _____ .

10. The songs _____ and _____ tell about Leadbelly's early working life in the fields of Louisiana and Texas.

11. The rhyme structure (give letters) for most 12-bar blues is _____ .

12. Leadbelly often played bass lines on his guitar that sounded a lot like the musical style known as _____ .

13. While living in Texas, Leadbelly hooked up with the country blues singer and guitar player _____ .

14. _____ and _____ are songs that reflect Leadbelly's prison experience.

15. Shortly after Leadbelly's death in New York, a folk group called the Weavers made his song _____ into a big hit.

16. Leadbelly's song about racial discrimination in Washington D.C. is called _____ .

THE NEW GENERATION QUIZ

Match the the information with the names at the right by placing the number in the blank.

Key		
13	___ former member of the Beach Boys	1. Bob Dylan
6	___ Indiana rocker	2. Arlo Guthrie
4	___ started with rhythm and blues	3. Emmylou Harris
12	___ *Will the Circle Be Unbroken*	4. Little Richard
5	___ interpreter of African-American roots music	5. Taj Mahal
1	___ "The Times They Are A-Changin'"	6. John Cougar Mellencamp
7	___ leader of "the outlaws" of country music	7. Willie Nelson
9	___ E Street Band	8. Pete Seeger
11	___ *The Joshua Tree*	9. Bruce Springsteen
1	___ "Mr. Tambourine Man"	10. Sweet Honey in The Rock
2	___ "Alice's Restaurant Massacree"	11. U2
10	___ unaccompanied singing	12. Doc Watson
3	___ country Grammy winner–"Blue Kentucky Girl"	13. Brian Wilson
8	___ "Turn, Turn, Turn"	
9	___ *Born in the U.S.A.*	
11	___ *Rattle and Hum*	
12	___ bluegrass flat-picked guitar	
1	___ from Duluth, Minnesota	
13	___ "Good Vibrations"	
4	___ "Good Golly, Miss Molly"	
7	___ "On the Road Again"	
2	___ sang Steve Goodman's "City of New Orleans"	
1	___ "A Hard Rain's A-Gonna Fall"	
4	___ Penniman from Macon, Georgia	
6	___ *Big Daddy*	
9	___ New Jersey "Boss" of mainstream rock	
10	___ Bernice Reagon and company	
11	___ from Ireland	
8	___ sang in the Weavers	
4	___ most outrageous singer of '50s rock 'n' roll	
5	___ plays piano, finger-style guitar, vibes, harmonica, banjo mandolin, bass and kalimba	
11	___ Paul "Bono" Hewson	
3	___ sang with Gram Parsons	
1	___ wrote "All Along the Watchtower"	